Managing Politics at Work

MANAGING POLITICS AT WORK

THE ESSENTIAL TOOLKIT FOR IDENTIFYING AND HANDLING POLITICAL BEHAVIOR IN THE WORKPLACE

Aryanne Oade

Director, Oade Associates Limited

palgrave
macmillan

First published 2009 by
PALGRAVE MACMILLAN

Palgrave Macmillan in the UK is an imprint of Macmillan Publishers Limited,
registered in England, company number 785998, of Houndmills, Basingstoke,
Hampshire RG21 6XS.

Palgrave Macmillan in the US is a division of St Martin's Press LLC,
175 Fifth Avenue, New York, NY 10010.

Palgrave Macmillan is the global academic imprint of the above companies
and has companies and representatives throughout the world.

Palgrave® and Macmillan® are registered trademarks in the United States,
the United Kingdom, Europe and other countries

ISBN-13: 978–0–230–59541–5
ISBN-10: 0–230–59541–3

This book is printed on paper suitable for recycling and made from fully
managed and sustained forest sources. Logging, pulping and manufacturing
processes are expected to conform to the environmental regulations of the
country of origin.

A catalogue record for this book is available from the British Library.

A catalog record for this book is available from the Library of Congress.

10 9 8 7 6 5 4 3 2 1
18 17 16 15 14 13 12 11 10 09

Printed and bound in China

Note from the Author

This book focuses on how you identify and manage other people's political behavior at work and, to some extent, how you manage your own political behavior as well. In writing the book, I am not seeking to advise you, the reader, on how to handle your workplace relationships, but rather to offer you my experiences and know-how as someone who has coached and worked with hundreds of clients on these issues. In addition to reading this book, you might want to seek the services and professional advice of a coach, business psychologist or consultant, each of whom should be able to offer you tailored, detailed and impartial counsel on the more challenging interpersonal and intrapersonal issues you might face at work.

Acknowledgments

I would like to acknowledge a number of people who have played a part in my work and the writing of this book.

Firstly, my thanks and gratitude go to all the clients who have spoken with me about their political experiences at work, sharing with me their successes, frustrations, reactions and strategies for managing – and using – political behavior in the workplace. These are perhaps the most stimulating and complex of issues to deal with and I have enjoyed every coaching meeting and workshop which focused on them.

Next, I like to thank the many clients and contacts who allowed me to pick their brains at the start of the writing process for this book. These conversations, about clients' and contacts' political experiences at work, were valuable in helping me make decisions about how to structure and focus the book. I am indebted to each of you and send my thanks to you gratefully and anonymously.

Also, my appreciation goes to my actor colleague Gina Rowland for her skills in re-creating believable business characters in coaching meetings, and for her helpful critique of seven chapters at the draft stage of the book; and to Eileen and Michael Scott for their timely and helpful review of Chapter 8.

Finally, I'm grateful to Stephen Rutt at Palgrave Macmillan for his speedy decision to publish this book and to the entire publishing team for being such effective and enjoyable co-workers.

Overview

WHAT THIS BOOK IS ABOUT

Politics at work is a fact of life. If you want to have influence in your workplace it is vital that you accurately identify, interpret and react to the political context around you. This is a book about how you handle politics in your workplace. The book focuses on how you manage the political situations and the political behavior you encounter at work. It is about your political behavior, and the political behavior used by the people you work with and for. It is also about the impact – productive, destructive and unexceptional – of political behaviors used by your colleagues and by you on other people, on yourself and on the department or team you work in. It is written for anyone who is struggling to understand, make sense of and respond effectively to the political context around them at work.

WHY I WROTE THIS BOOK

I wrote this book out of a firm conviction that how you behave at work – how you conduct yourself and handle other people – is what ultimately matters most. At the end of the day, it's the relationships that you build at work that count. It's not simply a matter of whether or not you possess the technical know-how your role requires. How you handle the people you work with is what will differentiate the adequate from the effective employee, and no more so than when other people's behavior – or your own – is partly or wholly motivated by political considerations. No matter how talented, intelligent, qualified or technically competent you are, without a comprehensive range of political skills – and more general people-handling skills – you won't perform as effectively as you could do in your role, you won't get the influence, promotion or projects you'd like and might well deserve, and you might not be seen as the effective, capable pair of hands your knowledge and technical skills suggest that you are.

MY BACKGROUND AND WORKPLACE POLITICAL EXPERIENCES

I am a Chartered Psychologist. I began working as a business psychologist in the late 1980s. During the following five years I worked for three consultancy firms. My experience of working for these firms was that I needed to expend much energy managing the relationships and political agendas of the people I worked alongside. I found myself as much a part of the political landscape as anyone else, and became caught up using political behavior as much as everybody else. I didn't like some of the behavior I saw around me, and I didn't like the fact that I ended up using some of it too. The working culture in each of these organizations was prevailingly political, and I found myself joining the party, much as I would have preferred to focus wholly on working productively with clients. Eventually, I wanted my energy and commitment to go solely toward delivering effective coaching programs and professional skills workshops. To that end I decided to work as an independent business psychologist.

Some of my initial projects were carried out as an associate to smaller consultancy firms. Then, in January 2000, I set up Oade Associates to design and deliver bespoke executive coaching programs, tailored professional skills workshops and custom-made conference scenarios. In this work I combine business psychology with the skills of professional actors to create real-life scenarios that reflect the leadership, management and political issues that my clients deal with in their work.

Since starting Oade Associates, I have run hundreds of executive coaching programs and professional skills workshops for managers and leaders working in the UK, Europe and North America. Many of these projects have involved working with clients on the reality of handling politics at work. In my coaching programs and workshops I ask clients to step back from their day-to-day work and political experiences. I ask them to reflect on the quality of the behavior they use when things are going well for them, and to compare that to what they do when they are under pressure. Then, with the help of my professional actor colleagues, I re-create the very meetings clients find most challenging – meetings which they mishandle or in which they lose influence or credibility – and help clients to revisit these meetings using different and more productive behavior, skills and interpersonal tactics. I coach them to understand the links between their intrapersonal world – their values, character and personality – and their interpersonal behavior: the tactics, skills and strategies they use with other people. Clients practise their new approaches until they are satisfied that they can go back to work and use them straightaway. As a result of working in this way clients perform better in their roles, have greater influence in their key workplace relationships and demonstrate sustained behavior change.

In addition to working one-to-one and with small groups I also work with conference audiences. In this case I develop a series of custom-made sketches which my actor colleagues subsequently enact live on stage. Audience members discuss and debate the action at round tables, so that they can learn from one another's experiences of handling similar instances and decide which interpersonal skills and tactics work well in particular situations and which don't. The scenarios can concentrate on any workplace issue, and recent sketches have focused on topics such as the politics surrounding working relationships and the politics of managing bullying and harassing behavior at work.

This book comes out of my work in helping clients to develop the political and people-handling skills they need to remain effective in highly political workplace environments – and it is informed by my own personal experiences of life as a consultancy employee.

How To Use This Book

WHO THIS BOOK IS FOR

A proportion of people go to work and look for opportunities to use political behavior. They regularly handle things in this way, prefer to do so and become adept at taking advantage of the dynamics they create when they work in this way. Many more of you, though, go to work focused primarily on using behavior which will enable you to get your job done, and which will result in you performing effectively in your role. You don't set out to be political: you set out to do a good job in a political environment.

You can find yourselves unhelpfully caught up in other people's political agendas. You consequently recognize that you will need, on occasion, to call upon political strategies of your own if you are to defend yourself, stand up for your rights, get the credit you deserve and have influence in key situations, even if you:

- Don't really want to act this way.
- Don't consider yourself skilled at doing so.
- Would really rather not do so.

When you do join the political sphere, you can find that the behaviors you choose in responding to the political ambitions of your colleagues don't always have the impact you'd expect them to have. Sometimes they are not effective at all. Sometimes they're only partially effective, reflecting the fact that you simply don't understand enough about the motivations of the protagonists or the dynamics of the situations they create. A lot of your time and effort goes into what are ultimately ineffective responses to the political strategies of others. I wrote this book for those of you who identify with this group of people.

I also wrote the book for those of you who don't feel equipped to engage with the politics you see going on around you at all, even when it directly, and unhelpfully, affects your work. You fear that, if you enter the mix, your more politically motivated and competent colleagues will not welcome your input and it will go badly for you. You lack the skills, confidence and know-how to enter the political arena safely, so you wait for your more politically accomplished colleagues to work it out between them, even though this means that you miss out on opportunities to influence the issues. If you had the mind-set and the capabilities of a more political operator you'd be able to speak up and have at least some influence in some situations. But lacking the capacity to enter the fray with any certainty – and afraid that if you do it'll backfire on you – you keep your head down and let others resolve the situations which evolve around you instead. I wrote this book for those of you who identify with this group of people too.

WHAT THIS BOOK WILL DO FOR YOU

This book will take you through a process of considering the political behavior you encounter and initiate in your workplace. It will help you reevaluate how well you respond to workplace politics and how productively you handle it. The book will introduce you to a series of six effective tools for managing workplace politics. Each tool stands alone or can be used in tandem with the other tools. Together they form a menu of options for you to draw on as you get to grips with the politics around you at work. Once you have been introduced to a tool, and worked through the exercises in the book related to it, you should be able to apply it to your working life straightaway.

The book will also introduce you to a series of case studies – and smaller examples – each of which mirrors realistic workplace political dynamics. A few of these scenarios are based on real-life incidents. In each of these instances the details of the characters, the setting of the events and the specific details of the scenarios have been fictionalized to protect the identities of the people involved. Each of the six main case studies is constructed to illustrate the themes of the chapter and tool preceding it. As you read a case study you will be asked to analyze it from the point of view of one or more of its key characters, applying the political tool from the preceding chapter to the action and finding solutions to the key political dynamics in the scenario.

Overall, the book will equip you with the insight, knowledge and tactics to enable you to:

- Gain and retain influence in political situations.
- Promote your interests, resolve conflicts, manage yourself and lead your team effectively when you are involved in – or feel the need to respond to – politically motivated agendas.
- Handle the political element you encounter at work with increased confidence and know-how.

Specifically the book will provide you with:

- Increased understanding about what motivates people in your workplace to adopt political strategies.
- Input to enable you to better analyze and identify political behavior at work.
- The knowledge, tools and tactics you need to help you manage your own and other people's political behavior more effectively.
- Insight into the impact of your own political behavior on your workplace contacts – and on your own reputation.
- Increased choices about how to conduct yourself and respond to other people at work, in situations where the political factor is a consideration.

STEPPING BACK FROM YOUR DAY-TO-DAY WORK

As you read the book you will be encouraged to step back from your day-to-day work and:

- Review how you currently manage workplace politics.
- Identify your areas of strength and your areas for development.
- Make decisions about what to do to improve the way in which you manage and handle the political element in your key business relationships.

YOUR RESPONSE TO POLITICAL BEHAVIOR

Even the most skilled people-handlers can founder when confronted with behavior that is political; behavior which is, by its very nature, not transparent, open and honest, and which, when tackled, doesn't respond to influence and dialog, doesn't follow the collaborative route even if it is presented as such, and is sometimes thought-provoking, possibly devious, often frustrating to deal with and, at times, simply divisive. Periodically, the book contains a series of questions for you to consider and answer in relation to your workplace political experiences and behavior. Each question is followed by a space in the text so that you can jot down your answers to it if you want to. These questions will provide you with an opportunity to apply the key points from the previous sections of the book to your working life, helping you get the most out of the process of reading the material.

This book will help you make the most of the political skills you've got. What a book like this can't do is make up for any lack of political intelligence you may have, or any lack of competency on your part in handling people. But it will show you how to handle the political element at your workplace more effectively, and should help you develop further political skills.

I am not advocating that every time you see an unhelpful political behavior, you should get involved and give a view. In every situation that you are tempted to engage with you will need to assess whether, given your seniority and the issues involved, it makes sense for you to do so. In some cases it may be unwise or foolhardy to act. But depending on the degree of political behavior in your organization, the issues involved and your influence in a given situation, it may be exactly the right thing to do.

YOUR POLITICAL BEHAVIOR AT WORK

The book is written to you, the reader, with the following note of caution. In my experience, when things go wrong for someone at work, it is unlikely to be because they are in the wrong job, although this is sometimes the case. It is much more likely that the person has neglected, or simply not managed, the human, political element of their work. They have not read the political landscape effectively enough. They have not considered deeply enough the political factors that matter to those with influence in a given situation. They haven't attended to the hidden agendas, personal dislikes, unresolved conflicts, power struggles and interpersonal dynamics that govern which decisions are made, by who, and when. My wish is that, with the help of this book, you will become more skilled, more effective and more productive at doing all these things, and that, in time, more and more of your energy and enthusiasm will go toward engaging with the aspects of your role that you find most rewarding, and less and less of your energy and enthusiasm will be dissipated responding ineffectively to other people's political activity.

Contents

start on their project immediately. This isn't the case, as work can only start once an account has been opened: a process that usually takes two weeks to complete. The case study centers on a meeting between the two salespeople and their two colleagues in Accounts Opening. A power struggle ensues whereby the two sales people try to intimidate their colleagues into making their work top priority, despite being told that it isn't possible to circumvent due diligence.

managers employ a range of political tactics which scapegoat the technology team in an attempt to cloud over the real issues: that they have failed to handle their responsibilities effectively and consequently have allowed service standards to slip.

CHAPTER 1

The Political Element at Work

Let's start with you and your experiences of politics in your workplace. We will go on to define political behavior at work shortly but, at the commencement of this first chapter, let's focus for a few minutes on:

- Your attitude to workplace political activity.
- The consequences you observe in your workplace of behavior which you consider to be politically motivated.

POLITICS: A FACT OF ORGANIZATIONAL LIFE

Political behavior at work is a fact of life. You will encounter it everywhere, in your team, your department or group, in your managers, your peers, in those who work for you and in yourself. Depending on how prevalent political conduct is in your workplace you may find that some, or maybe most, of the decisions made by your leaders and managers, and many of the decisions that you make yourself, are influenced by political considerations. Whatever your view of workplace political activity, it is something you need to get to grips with.

Many of you reading this book may be doing so because you want to learn how to handle the politics in your workplace more effectively. You want to learn how to identify and engage with the political agendas around you without either shooting yourself in the foot or making a challenging situation worse. You want to acquire additional insight, tools, knowledge and wisdom to help you navigate political territory effectively, and to enable you to have a positive impact on potentially tricky circumstances. You want to learn how to refocus politically motivated agendas on to the true business issues that need to be addressed and learn how to manage workplace relationships with your more politically minded colleagues more effectively.

Others of you may be reading this book because you are fed up of workplace politics. You see it as a pointless waste of time. You may make observations about how prevalent politics is in your organization, and how it gets in the way of you and many of your colleagues doing your jobs properly. You may comment on how annoying and energy sapping it can be. You may see political activity as something that takes up precious time, but doesn't achieve anything beyond the self-advancement of certain key players. Part of you wants to shout with frustration and tell them all to get on with their real jobs. In reading this book, you are looking for pointers about why people behave in ways which you find worthless; you'd like to understand what it is that motivates some of your colleagues to invest so much time and effort in pursuit of goals that seem inconsequential to you.

So, just what is your attitude to workplace politics? You might like to take a few minutes to jot down what you think of it in the space below:

NOT ENGAGING WITH WORKPLACE POLITICS

Whatever you have written, and however skeptically or pragmatically you view workplace politicking, you may have difficulty engaging with it. Those of you who choose not to get involved in many of the situations at work that you consider to be politically motivated may have some good reasons for not doing so. What are they? You might like to jot down some of them in the space below:

You might now like to compare your list with the points below which reflect some of the most common reasons why people prefer not to engage with workplace politics. It may be that you:

- Don't know how to have a positive impact.
- Feel powerless to do anything effective.
- Lack the seniority to feel safe enough to get involved.
- Are intimidated by your more robust and ambitious colleagues.
- Worry that, if you do get involved, you'll mess up and you'd have been better off not getting involved in the first place.

There are very real risks inherent in wading into a sensitive political arena and upsetting people with more organizational clout, influence and authority than you; people whose subsequent opinion of you can change for the worse and whose view of you could adversely affect your career going forward. But, there are also many benefits to having the skills, sensitivity, interpersonal acumen and political know-how that mean you can make a contribution, however small or large, when you want to.

THE CONSEQUENCES OF POLITICS AT YOUR WORKPLACE

Every organization has its own distinct political character, and the political dynamics in your workplace will be unique to it. I'd like you to consider the character of the political activity you encounter in your place of work. You might like to take a few minutes to jot down a list of what you consider to be the consequences of the politics you observe around you at work. You can use the space below to write down your thoughts:

You might now like to compare your list with the points below which outline some of the commonly cited consequences of workplace politics:

- Ill-thought out decisions.
- Decisions made on the basis of only one consideration, such as finance.
- Petty competition between colleagues, teams or departments.
- People feeling they have little or no control over decisions that affect them.
- Missed opportunities to collaborate.
- Escalated conflicts, unnecessary aggression and arguments.
- Missed deadlines.
- Wasted resources, errors and rework.
- Dissatisfied customers, reduced profits.
- Disheartened and, sometimes, demoralized employees.

All of these consequences are negative. Rarely does anyone comment that one of the outcomes of political behavior at work is that it enhances their workplace, causes more effective decisions to be made and raises profits. It is seen, usually, as a counterproductive aspect of organizational life, but, nonetheless, it is also seen as a universal fact of organizational life. So if you want to be able to influence key issues in your workplace – or simply those that relate directly to your work – you will need to develop the capacity to engage with the often challenging political context around you.

THE STARTING POINT FOR HANDLING POLITICS

Understanding the political agendas, motivations and behaviors of key players at work – and responding effectively to them – is the starting point if you want to have genuine influence in your workplace. You need to be able to read the political agendas that matter, understand the issues from the point of view of the key protagonists and be prepared to adopt effective, sensitive political approaches as and when you need them. You need to know how to identify, handle, respond to and, at times, initiate effective political strategies at work.

So whether you are stepping into political waters for the first time, or you are used to the political context and already skilled at some aspects of political management, the rest of this book will provide you with insight into what constitutes political behavior at work, will help you examine the nature of political activity in your workplace in more depth, and will outline for you an effective set of skills, tactics and tools that you can adopt, use and develop to give you more options when you encounter other people's political tactics and want to have influence in the situation.

SUMMARY AND NEXT CHAPTER

So far we have considered your attitude to workplace politics and the impact on you of the workplace political activity you encounter. Let's now turn our attention to defining what constitutes political behavior at work and identify some of the key traits associated with it.

A Definition of Politically Motivated Behavior

Let's now turn our attention to defining what 'political behavior at work' actually means. Everyone has a view about what constitutes political activity in the workplace. So let's explore your perspective on it, define it, and examine some examples of what might constitute political and nonpolitical behavior at work, before giving you an opportunity to assess your own political behavior on a key workplace issue.

The aim of this chapter is to give you a workable and straightforward way of identifying what does and what does not constitute political behavior at work, so that, when you do come across it, you are better prepared to recognize it and handle it effectively.

WHAT IS POLITICAL BEHAVIOR AT WORK?

What does the term 'political behavior at work' mean to you? You might like to use the following space to jot down your top of the head reaction to this term, noting what words, phrases and associations it conjures up for you:

You might now like to compare your list with the points below, which, while not intended to be an exhaustive list, outlines some of the commonly cited responses to the question you just answered:

- Hidden agendas.
- Power struggles.
- Egos and ambitions.
- Personal animosities.
- Power retained in the hands of only a few people.
- Issues presented in one way when they're really about something else.
- Personal agendas.
- Managing other people's perceptions.
- Taking credit for someone else's work.
- Jockeying for position and trying to impress the boss.
- Basic discourtesy and impoliteness.

The challenge of identifying and managing other people's political behavior at work lies in the fact that, much of the time, in assessing what does constitute a politically motivated behavior and what does not, you have to make judgments about other people's intentions based on:

- Their observed behavior.
- The context surrounding that behavior.
- Your understanding of what they want to achieve.

In any given situation you may only have partial knowledge of any of these three things, and, in some circumstances, only the observed behavior to go on. So, if you are going to accurately identify an observed behavior as being 'a political behavior', rather than simply a nonpolitical one, what criteria are you going to use to help you make this distinction?

POLITICAL BEHAVIOR AT WORK: A DEFINITION

Consider the following definition which captures some of the key elements – for me at least – of the term 'political behavior at work'. Political behavior at work is about:

- The degree to which a person's workplace activity is directed toward meeting their own internal agenda, *where that agenda takes them away from working toward the stated goals associated with their role*. In other words, they put their own personal considerations (for instance their needs, wishes, values, preferences, likes, dislikes, animosities) above any other consideration (for instance customer requirements, collaborating effectively with colleagues, resolution of conflicts, shared decision making) when making decisions and carrying out their workplace duties.
- The fact that the person using the political behavior is likely to be doing so to gain something – power or control or kudos or credit – *without being transparent and open about what they want or what they are doing*.

AN EXAMPLE OF POLITICAL BEHAVIOR

Consider this example – of a facilities manager allocating her departmental budget – and the two possible scenarios that follow. Here we are looking at the difference between a manager acting within her role goals and one behaving politically.

A facilities manager in a large organization works hard to acquire increased budget. Her department has recently received poor feedback from all of its key internal client groups. She puts together a business case for increased spend and arranges a series of meetings with her peers and senior managers to outline what she will do with the increased budget and why it should come to her and her department. She says the additional budget is necessary to help her improve service delivery to all her internal client groups. As her department has a key role to play in the service delivery chain she eventually prevails. After several weeks of debate and discussion she succeeds in making her case and is given additional budget:

- When she gets the increased budget she immediately sends her staff on customer service workshops. She then sets up a series of meetings with her internal client groups to improve the quality of communication between them and her own group. At these meetings, despite knowing it will inevitably cause short-term discomfort for her and her team, the manager asks her internal clients for feedback on what her group is doing to meet their expectations, and on what they are not doing well enough to meet their requirements. At the meetings, she and her senior staff work hard to listen to the feedback, and subsequently make changes which bring service standards more in line with clients' expectations. It is a very difficult time for the whole department, with some members of staff commenting bitterly that their manager has encouraged complaints to be made about the team by its customers, and has left them wide open to criticism and adverse comment.

- When she gets her increased budget she asks one of her staff to research relevant customer service workshops, but never actually commits to sending any of her team on them. When subsequently asked by a peer about the reasons for the delay in getting her staff trained she stalls, saying that she has other 'pressing team issues' to deal with first. She stalls again when she subsequently says that 'it'd be in the best interests of her group' if she spent the money in 'a more cost-effective way', but gives no details about what she means by this. After several weeks, and when the dust has settled, she starts to suggest to her peers that she could use her new budget in cross-departmental initiatives. She lets it be known that if they support her proposals on key issues, she will make the budget available to a wider audience than simply her own department.

Example One: Analyzing the Political Dynamics

Let's consider what has happened in these two scenarios, starting with the first one. The manager in this scenario is not politically motivated in this instance, and is using transparent means to achieve her role goals. She:

- Says she wants the additional budget to improve service delivery.
- Sends her staff on customer service workshops.
- Sets up meetings with her internal clients to identify delivery improvements.
- Implements suitable changes in her department.
- Takes considerable flak from her staff for leaving them exposed to criticism by clients.

It is a painful time for her and her department, but, in the end, it is worth it. Throughout the scenario the manager takes actions that are in keeping with her role goals: that of improving the standard of service her group offers to its internal clients. Any of her colleagues observing her conduct throughout this period would not find any discrepancy between:

- Her observed behavior (requesting and using increased budget to create service improvements).
- The context surrounding that behavior (poor feedback from internal client groups).
- Their understanding of what she wants to achieve (to improve service delivery standards).

In the second instance the manager is acting politically throughout. She lets her true, hidden wish – to use increased budget as a bargaining tool with her peer group – dominate the way in which she handles her senior managers, her peers, her team, her customers and her budget. She conceals this hidden agenda and instead she:

- Tells her managers and peers that she wants the budget to improve service delivery – but then does not spend the money in this way when she has the opportunity to do so.
- Raises her staff's expectations that they will receive customer service training – but doesn't provide them with it.
- Leads her clients to believe that she will take concrete steps toward improving customer service standards – but doesn't do anything toward this aim.

- Creates fog when asked by her peer why she hasn't spent the money on customer-service training for her staff – and gives a vague and misleading response.
- Lies by saying that she will use the money in a more cost-effective way – when she doesn't have anything concrete in mind.
- Tries, eventually, to use the budget to trade favours with her peers – which is a reflection of her real, hidden agenda.

Any of her colleagues observing her conduct throughout this period will find several discrepancies between:

- Her observed behavior (requesting increased budget to create service improvements).
- The context surrounding that behavior (poor feedback from internal client groups and her stated desire to address these issues).
- Their understanding of what she wants to achieve (she says one thing and does another, so from her behavior it isn't clear what she wants to achieve: at every turn she doesn't act in line with what she says she wants to do. Ultimately, she doesn't take any actions in keeping with her stated objective: to improve service delivery).

This manager does not do what she says she will do, and the actions she takes are not in keeping with her role goals. Throughout the scenario what the manager really wants is to secure bargaining power with her peer group. Her way of securing this goal is, however, indirect. Her desire to have influence with her peer group is understandable and not reprehensible at all. But the methods she employs to achieve this goal are: she conceals her true motives, lies, misrepresents her need for additional budget and misleads her staff, clients, peers and managers.

POLITICAL BEHAVIOR: A HIGH PRICE TO PAY?

Looking at this example, you may think that this manager is taking a significantly high reputational risk by using the political approach she chooses. She runs the risk of harming her reputation in the eyes of her staff, clients, peers and managers. What might motivate her to take these risks?

Every person is unique and has their own reasons for behaving at work as they do. But, it is likely that people who use destructive political behavior continually, and seem blind to the consequences they create for themselves and others, probably don't readily make the connection between their behavior and not being well thought of. They simply don't see it this way, preferring instead to see themselves as people using behavior which is justifiable, even necessary, given the environment in which they work.

Bearing in mind that each person's political motivations are unique I think that habitual political operators, like the second manager cited in the example above, often feel – deep down inside – powerless interpersonally, and use the tactics they do because they think that these strategies will help them get what they want. What this manager has failed to see is that the tactics she uses actually create a dynamic in her relationships which means that her colleagues:

- Do become wary of her.
- Don't fully trust her.
- Don't want to be that closely involved in her work.

She fails to see that the political agenda she pursues makes it more likely that she will get left out of information-giving and decision-making loops, and makes it more likely that when she has a problem few people will want to help her resolve it. Without the support of her colleagues she *will* become, to some extent, powerless at work and, feeling powerless, might well resort to political tactics again and again, perpetuating the cycle.

However, should this manager ever confront her own inner motives and fears, and start to use more open and transparent behavior, she might start to build genuinely co-operative and effective relationships at work, relationships which make it more likely that others will work with her, will include her in information-giving and decision-making loops and will work with her to achieve mutual goals.

WHAT CONSTITUTES NONPOLITICAL BEHAVIOR?

We have just considered a definition of political behavior at work. We now need to clarify what kinds of behavior are excluded from this definition, no matter how challenging they might be to deal with at the time. In other words, we need to clarify which behaviors, even if they are demanding and tricky to deal with, annoying and vexing, are not, actually, politically motivated. These include:

- Disagreements or arguments between your colleagues about what your team or your organization's goals should be.
- Disagreements or arguments between your colleagues about what constitutes a fact, or what weight should be given to certain facts.

- Differences of opinion, even passionate differences of opinion, between your colleagues about what values matter at work: say in the way your organization treats its employees or customers, or the way in which two or three people are going to work together.
- Differences of opinion, even ardent ones, between colleagues about what procedures, processes, strategies or tactics are most likely to achieve your organization's goals, your team's objectives or your desired outcome on a piece of work being jointly handled by two or more people.

These are all part and parcel of everyday organizational life, and do not in and of themselves, constitute political activity; except, that is, when one of your colleagues – or you – decides to use these discussions for political purposes.

Consider the following example which describes a second instance of political behavior, as well as describing a clear case of behavior which is nonpolitical, but still highly taxing to deal with.

AN EXAMPLE OF NONPOLITICAL BEHAVIOR

The Director of Programming for an independent film production company decides to make a series of films about sports stars as role models. He asks a well-known television sports commentator to write the voice-over script for the first program, which will focus on European professional footballers. The program will highlight the pressure on these high profile sportsmen to become role models for younger fans. The sports commentator likes the suggestion for the program, accepts the commission and, not having met the Director of Programming before, places a telephone call to him to talk about his preliminary ideas for the voice-over script. The sports commentator suggests that he write a first draft and then hand it across to the Director of Programming for comment, before proceeding to finalize the script based on his feedback.

- The Director of Programming says that he would like to have a look at the first draft, and would then like to work with the sports commentator, step by step, to explain his feedback and discuss it with him. He agrees, produces the first draft and sends it across to the Director of Programming. The Director of Programming has many changes and suggestions to make and the sports commentator is surprised at the scale and number of alterations he proposes. However, when discussing his amendments with the sports commentator, the Director of Programming makes it clear why he wants to make a particular change and in what way his suggested alterations will add value to the script. He usually, but not always, persuades the sports commentator that he has something valuable to add, and when they remain in disagreement, even after protracted debate, the sports commentator respects that it is ultimately the Director of Programming's call. The sports commentator isn't used to having his work criticized as frequently as this. At various stages of the feedback he feels angry, picked on and got at, and even has to bite his tongue once or twice. But he does learn a lot from the Director of Programming about how to structure, frame and write an effective voice-over script. The Director of Programming's manner throughout his dealings with the sports commentator is business-like, even crisp, but he always returns his calls and emails, even if there is sometimes a delay in him responding.

■ The Director of Programming makes it clear that whatever the sports commentator writes in his first draft, he will have absolute discretion over the final content of the script. The sports commentator is somewhat taken aback and suggests that the two of them should agree on any changes one by one. The Director of Programming swiftly counters by saying that he will have complete editorial control over the final script. His tone is absolute, and the sports commentator concludes that he might be tricky to deal with. The sports commentator ends the call and considers pulling out of the assignment. In the end, however, he writes the script over the next few days and sends it to the Director of Programming. The Director of Programming's initial feedback surprises and disappoints the sports commentator, being both superficial and sparse. It doesn't deal with substantial issues such as the content, tone or quality of the script, only with the Director of Programming's view that the sports commentator needs to use shorter sentences, and shorter words, as the program is aimed at a younger audience. Subsequently when the sports commentator contacts the Director of Programming again to discuss various issues about the content and recording of the program, he is surprised to find that the Director of Programming randomly ignores some calls and only returns some emails. On one occasion, the Director of Programming doesn't turn up for a scheduled telephone call *he* had arranged with the sports commentator. The sports commentator emails him straightaway, reminding him about the scheduled meeting. The following morning the Director of Programming replies claiming that he had been busy, but not apologizing or offering to rearrange the telephone meeting. The script was used on the program and with fewer changes than the sports commentator feared, but without any substantial improvements being made to it either. None of the few alterations that were made was discussed with him beforehand.

Example Two: Analyzing the Political Dynamics

Let's consider what has happened in these two scenarios, starting with the first one. In the first scenario the Director of Programming is not acting politically. His sole aim is to make changes to the script which will improve it. His motive is to make the script a better script and he is quite determined in pursuing this aim. He:

- Makes numerous changes to the text, but takes the time to explain each one to the sports commentator, outlining why each change is an important change to make.
- Doesn't desist even when it is clear his feedback is annoying the sports commentator: he is committed to his goal of improving the quality of the script.
- Always returns the sports commentator's emails and phone calls, signaling that he wants to collaborate with the sports commentator's agenda and the issues he raises, as well as pursuing his own agenda.

His overall approach is one characterized by a willingness to invest time in his relationship with the sports commentator. He preserves the quality of his dialog with him, despite wanting to rewrite much of what he has written in his script, because he treats him as an equal, even though he is businesslike and crisp when speaking with him.

In the second scenario the Director of Programming is politically motivated. He uses his position in the film production company as a justification for adopting a directive approach to the sports commentator, simply so that he can feel in control. He:

- Insists on the right to alter whatever he has written, in any way he wants, without necessarily discussing it with the sports commentator beforehand.
- Misses a telephone meeting he schedules with the sports commentator, subsequently claiming to be busy with important issues that took precedence over the call.
- Demonstrates basic discourtesy in randomly disregarding some of his emails and telephone messages, signaling that he regards many of the issues the sports commentator wishes to raise with him as unimportant and that, when he does respond to a message, it will be on his terms and in response to his agenda only.

- Gives minimal and cursory feedback on his script to the sports commentator.
- Doesn't discuss any of the changes he does make to the script with the sports commentator before making the program.

His overall approach is one characterized by an autocratic and unilateral approach to managing his relationship with the sports commentator. He patronizes him in order to signal to him that, as far as he is concerned, he is in charge.

Although the two Directors of Programming want the same thing – the right to make changes to the text written by the sports commentator before recording the script – their reasons for doing so are very different. The first Director of Programming is a demanding and tough professional who wants to make the best program he can. He reads the first draft of the script thoroughly and devises many changes to it to improve its quality. The changes he suggests are genuine changes, prompted by his belief that he can see a more effective way to write the script. This is an example of a nonpolitical, professional behavior, highly challenging though it is for the sports commentator to deal with.

The second Director of Programming is a very different character. He needs to feel in control and therefore wants his opinions to go unchallenged. He wants the sports commentator to defer to his will in every change he wants to make, not because the changes he suggests will necessarily improve the quality of the script – although they might – or because he has made a compelling case for any of the changes he proposes. His reason for wanting absolute control over what is in the script is that it gives him the illusion of being in control. He lets his internal agenda – to feel powerful, in control and a specialist in his field – dominate all other considerations in his dealings with the sports commentator, considerations such as treating him with professional courtesy or responding to all of his calls or explaining why he wants to alter his script.

This is an example of a political, and highly challenging, behavior to deal with. If the sports commentator takes the Director of Programming's behavior at face value, and believes he is genuinely too busy to deal effectively with his queries, he will continue to handle him in the same open and collaborative way as he started off. This will result in him losing power in the relationship and the Director of Programming will gain the upper hand. The sports commentator will have a very hard time working with him. In order to get any sort of dialog going with him, and get his input to the issues that matter to him, the sports commentator will have to change tack.

Later chapters of this book will help you decide what you could do if you find yourself in his shoes.

YOUR POLITICAL BEHAVIOR

Having taken a look at what does and what does not constitute political behavior at work, I'd like you now to step back and take a look at your own political behavior in the workplace. Consider the following framework. It identifies, at a high level, four stances that you could adopt to a particular workplace issue based on your:

- Motivation to achieve the goals associated with your role on that issue.
- Skills at influencing other people on that issue.

The framework I have devised wants you to make a conscious connection between your motivation and the quality of your influencing skills to form a judgment about whether you think your political activity is constructive or destructive to you and to your employing organization on that issue. The framework is issue driven, so it is quite possible for you to behave as a constructive influencer on one issue, and as a destructive employee on another; or as a well-intentioned but ineffective influencer on one issue and as an undermining employee on another.

So identify an issue at work that matters to you and that you are currently engaged in handling – or have recently ceased handling. Consider your conduct in relation to that issue in the light of Figure 2.1.

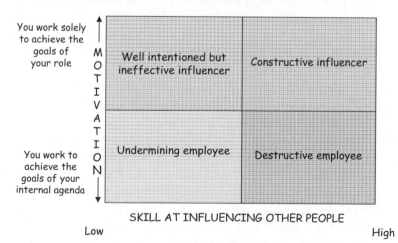

Figure 2.1 Political agendas that people adopt at work   Aryanne Oade (2009)

- Constructive influencer: If you see yourself as a constructive influencer then you think you are adept at using your well-developed influencing skills in pursuit of your role goals on this issue. You see yourself as someone who reads the political landscape well. You think you are able to influence key people in ways that are helpful to you achieving your role goals on this issue. You think that you make a helpful contribution to your team or organization and are actively involved in activity which will help you achieve your role goals and objectives. Your main effort at work is directed toward achieving the goals associated with your role and not toward achieving internal agendas of your own. You work in ways that your colleagues would see as open, transparent and effective.

- Destructive employee: If you see yourself as a destructive employee then you want to use your well-developed influencing skills to help you achieve your own internal agenda on this issue. This could be any number of things: only you will know. Your main effort on this issue goes toward achieving the aims of your internal, hidden agenda. It follows that you might hinder the part of your employing organization over which you have influence from achieving its stated goals and objectives on this issue. Why? Because your main aim is not to raise the quality of your products or services, or to listen to your customers, or to improve business relationships with your peers or to work more productively with your seniors *even if you claim it is*. Your main aim is internal to you, and it is likely to be the real driver behind your decisions and actions. If, for instance, it is to acquire and retain organizational power then what you really want is to have power over people and issues, rather than to use the power available to you in your role to help your team or organization better meet its goals and objectives. Usually your activity is at odds with your real job description, no matter how you choose to present it. You are likely to employ any number of the political behaviors identified earlier in the chapter, and the quality of your relationships with your colleagues will reflect your indirect and possibly manipulative methods.

- Well-intentioned but ineffective influencer: If you see yourself in the top left quadrant, you want to make a genuine contribution to your team or organization by achieving the goals associated with your role on this issue, but you lack the influencing skills to do so. You will need to develop a suite of influencing and political management skills, skills that enable you to build and sustain effective relationships with your key business contacts. You may want to consider improving your ability to read other peoples' styles and your ability to flex your style with the different styles other people use. You may want to develop the capacity to handle and resolve conflict. You will need a professional skills toolkit that will enable you to work constructively with other people in your workplace and which will bring you the influence you'd like to have. You should find some of the input you need in the following chapters in this book, but you may need to look for other sources of development as well.

- Undermining employee: If you see yourself in the bottom left quadrant then you'd like to pursue your own hidden agenda on this issue but aren't skilled at achieving this aim. You are likely to engage in activity that undermines both yourself and your organization, activity that has nothing to do with either your role goals or your team or organization's objectives. Your poor influencing skills prevent you from gaining the organizational influence you'd like to have and ultimately you may gain a reputation as someone who shoots themselves in the foot, undermining both themselves and their employer in the process. It is likely that people see through your attempts to use political behavior and may avoid dealing with you where possible to make their lives easier. Knowing that you currently play it this way, you need to ask yourself, 'how long am I going to continue to undermine myself?' In my opinion, people who concentrate on gaining the skills and wisdom of a constructive influencer are always the ones who end up with genuine, real organizational weight. The power they have is that of the authentic influence that comes from being skilled at working with other people openly and transparently, and thereby gaining the respect of colleagues and customers. If you see yourself in the bottom left quadrant you may want to think seriously about changing your values and acquiring the skills by which to work in more transparent, influential and open ways.

SUMMARY AND THE NEXT CHAPTER

This chapter has focused on:

- Reviewing what 'political behavior at work' means to you.
- Defining workplace political behavior and some of the traits associated with it.
- Exploring an example of political behavior in the facilities department of a large organization.
- Examining what constitutes nonpolitical behavior with an example set in the independent film production industry.

- Providing you with an opportunity to asses the quality of your own political behavior on a recent or current issue at work.

The following case study illustrates these themes further. It focuses on the relationship between two nonpolitically minded team members and their politically minded manager. The case study centers on what happens when a team member fails to read the political intent of her manager, consequently mishandles her, and then loses out when the boss decides to move a potentially high earning account from her and give it to her peer.

Switching Accounts

BACKGROUND AND CHARACTERS

This case study is set in the offices of a global media and communications company in Amsterdam, The Netherlands. The company is divided into geographic regions and Henriette is head of The Netherlands, Belgium, Northern France and Luxemburg. Her clients range from major hotel chains to motor manufacturers and department stores. Henriette has run her region for two years, during which time there has been a small increase in client revenues. She has made it an ambition of hers to double revenues in the next five years, and has publicized this target throughout the region.

Henriette has a team of 11 people working for her. She works long hours and expects her team to do so as well. Her management style involves engendering competition among her team members. She sees this feature of her style as positive. She believes it creates an atmosphere of healthy competition between able-minded people, and that it incentivizes and rewards top performers. She doesn't agree with the view that this method of incentivizing co-workers is potentially divisive and might undermine relationships between colleagues who work alongside one another. Henriette prefers the view that independent self-starters know how to handle themselves and understand that to succeed they need to work hard, be ruthless if necessary and, ultimately, stand alone. Henriette is quick to judge people, and is slow to forgive what she regards as failure or underperformance. She can be, by turns, manipulative and bullying, and can literally ignore people she dislikes or disrespects, while using charming and warm behavior with those in her team of whom she approves. Henriette has a positive profile in the wider company. She has developed a reputation for being engaging, charismatic and effective. She is popular with clients who regard her as being responsive, knowledgeable, committed to their welfare and someone who delivers.

Nellie has worked for Henriette for seven months, following a transfer from the Scandinavian offices of the company. Nellie was offered a move to Henriette's region in order to give her greater experience in different parts of the European business. Her initial reaction on being offered the move was one of hesitancy. She felt ambivalent about working for a woman with a reputation for being periodically fierce and not that supportive of her staff. However, Nellie's mentor suggested that she should take the opportunity to work for someone with a different style to her own in order to learn from her and round out her experience. Nellie is a friendly, co-operative, hard-working and committed employee. She is ambitious and not politically minded. She is by nature supportive, and wants to build and maintain productive relationships with her colleagues and her manager. On her first day in Henriette's region, her new manager handed Nellie a series of files on dormant accounts. Henriette did not offer to introduce Nellie to her new colleagues, nor did she react well to Nellie's suggestion that Henriette fill her in on the background to the accounts she had been given or the events which had resulted in the accounts becoming dormant. Henriette tells Nellie that she must stand on her own two feet and that she doesn't have time for hand-holding. Henriette doesn't particularly want to crush her new team member; more so tell her how it is and make it clear that she respects autonomy and decisiveness. While concerned that Nellie might be a bit touchy-feely for her liking, she is actually open-minded about whether or not her new team member will become a valuable member of the team – but Nellie could have been forgiven for not realizing this.

Dirkje has worked for Henriette for nearly three years. Initially, he found it challenging and draining working for someone with so few people-handling skills and such little empathy for other people in the team. However, he has learned how to handle Henriette and is effective at creating an impression she likes; he doesn't challenge her, works hard, gets results and gives her the credit where he can. Dirkje basically likes people and is able interpersonally. He is naturally tactful and sociable, doesn't need or want much structure to his work and likes the freedom and independence that Henriette gives to her team members. Being resourceful and flexible Dirkje has done well in the team and Henriette tends to delegate more work to him than to anyone else in her region.

NELLIE'S FIRST MONTH

Nellie steps back from Henriette during her first month. She observes her new manager dealing with her colleagues in the office, attends presentations she gives in the region and forms a view about her manager's character. Nellie sees Henriette as someone who engenders great personal loyalty among some team members. But she also sees Henriette as someone who takes a strong dislike to some people while making life unnecessarily hard for others. She is very committed to the company and sets high standards. This is all fine with Nellie who is ambitious herself, but she is worried about Henriette's tactics as a manager; she withholds information, takes the credit for other people's achievements and lies to cover her own back when things go wrong. Nellie has a strong preference for working for a supportive boss, and she fairs better in co-operative workplace relationships. Ideally, she'd prefer her boss to be her coach too, but, realizing that Henriette is not cut from that cloth, she sets out to do the very best she can to turn around the dormant accounts and win her manager's respect through her achievements.

Nellie sets about this task positively. She sees it as a challenge to turn dormant accounts into fee-earning accounts – after all, these clients must, at some time, have done business with the company – and quickly focuses on re-engaging with a hotel chain. She researches into the history of the company's dealings with the hotel chain, contacts them, gives her manager periodic updates and, after a number of telephone calls and exchanges with the hotel chain's marketing manager, arranges a meeting to discuss how her company can support them going forward.

NELLIE'S SECOND AND THIRD MONTHS

Nellie is hopeful that she will, after all, be able to win the hotel chain back to her company. She is up against two rival firms and, after much hard work, is shortlisted along with one of the other companies, for a sizable piece of business. She is delighted to have secured this opportunity after a relatively short period of time working to reopen dormant accounts and tells Henriette the good news. Dirkje notices how hard Nellie is working and comments to her that she is burning the candle at both ends. They go for a beer to celebrate the good news of the opportunity to bring the hotel chain back to the firm.

NELLIE'S FOURTH AND FIFTH MONTHS

Sadly for her, Nellie doesn't prevail. She loses, narrowly, to the rival company and is dismayed that, while she came close, she didn't manage to re-engage the hotel chain. She is even more dismayed at the prospect of telling Henriette the bad news. Before going to see her boss she tells Dirkje what has happened and that she now has to go and relay the news to Henriette. Dirkje tells her not to worry, that her boss will understand: everyone can see how hard she has worked.

Nellie goes to see her manager, and, having been influenced by Dirkje's optimistic appraisal of their manager's likely reaction, expects some understanding. She reminds Henriette how many hours she has put into the project and, that even though she hasn't succeeded this time, points out that she has learned a lot and demonstrated her dedication and commitment to the cause. However, Henriette isn't at all sympathetic and comments coldly that Nellie has 'failed to secure a good return on her investment of the company's time in the project' before walking away without offering either support or commiseration.

NELLIE'S SIXTH MONTH

Henriette calls a team meeting and asks each team member to update her on where they have got to with their various projects. When it is Nellie's turn to speak she informs her boss that she is close to reopening their dormant account with a French cosmetics firm, and suggests that she will have more information by the end of the week. Henriette's response is to tell Nellie that she cannot make their scheduled one-to-one meeting at 4 pm that afternoon, a comment she utters with devastating coldness.

Two days later Henriette calls Nellie and Dirkje into her office and tells them that she is taking the cosmetic company account away from Nellie and giving it to Dirkje. She explains that she wants to move various accounts around in order to maximize revenues for the company. Nellie complains that she is close to reopening the account, has worked long and hard on the project, and that moving it to another colleague at this stage may injure the relationship between the client and the company, but Henriette doesn't listen. She smoothly explains that in a meritocracy the top earners need to be incentivized. She turns to Dirkje and asks for his reaction to the news. He likes Nellie but he isn't about to look a gift horse in the mouth. In front of his boss he makes the right noises, which leaves Nellie stunned and defeated.

ANALYZING THE POLITICAL DYNAMICS: YOUR ROLE

Consider the following questions. They are designed to help you look behind the facts of the case study and examine the political dynamics at play between Henriette, Nellie and Dirkje. You can jot down your answers to each question in the space below it. The first set of questions invite you to analyze the political dynamics from Nellie's viewpoint:

- Nellie mishandles her manager Henriette from their first meeting. Accepting that she is difficult to work for what mistakes does Nellie make?

- Nellie doesn't manage to win the hotel chain back to the company. What mistakes does she make when relaying this information to her boss?

- During the team update meeting that Henriette calls, she is cold and cutting with Nellie in front of the whole team. How should Nellie have interpreted this behavior?

- Henriette removes Nellie's cosmetics account from her and gives it to Dirkje on the pretext of incentivizing top performers. Nellie doesn't react effectively this time either. What could she have done to try and salvage this situation?

The next set of questions invites you to analyze the political dynamics from Dirkje's viewpoint:

- Dirkje has learned how to handle Henriette. Given the definition of political behavior introduced in the previous chapter, to what extent is his decision to adopt behavior his boss approves of political tactic on his part?

▪ Dirkje accepts the removal of the cosmetics company from Nellie and its placement with him. To what extent does this represent a betrayal of his relationship with Nellie?

> [blank box]

The next set of questions invites you to analyze the political issues surrounding Henriette's approach to managing her two team members Nellie and Dirkje:

▪ Henriette decides to remove Nellie's cosmetics account from her and give it to Dirkje on the pretext of incentivizing him. What is her real motivation for this maneuver?

> [blank box]

▪ Given the definitions of political behavior introduced in the previous chapter, to what extent is Henriette's behavior toward Nellie at this point politically motivated?

> [blank box]

The last question invites you to reflect on how a clearer understanding of her boss's political intent could have helped Nellie from the outset:

▪ Nellie could have handled her manager so that, despite failing to win back the hotel chain, she might have continued her work with the cosmetics company. Given the definition of political behavior introduced in the previous chapter, how would a clearer understanding of her boss's political mindedness have helped Nellie handle her more skilfully?

> [blank box]

LEARNING FROM NELLIE'S MISTAKES

The final section of this chapter provides a summary of the key issues that Nellie mishandles. Each of the bullet points below relates, in order, to each of the questions above. You might like to read each answer and compare it with the notes that you jotted down. Let's look at the political issues from Nellie's viewpoint first:

■ Nellie mishandles her manager Henriette from their first meeting. Accepting that she is difficult to work for what mistakes does Nellie make?

During their six months working together Nellie doesn't realize just how political her manager is. Even after their curt meeting on her first day, Nellie fails to realize that Henriette has only one mode of handling her staff and is always in that mode. Being a more relational and less political character, Nellie doesn't really clue in to the fact that her boss is both hard-nosed and a political operator. Because she doesn't recognize her for what she is, Nellie misses the very real signals that Henriette gives her throughout their time working together, and so mismanages her relationship with her from day one. Nellie does recognize that her boss operates from a different paradigm to her, but she fails to understand the extent of their differences. Nellie's first mistake is that she doesn't really hear what her boss means when she tells her on her first day that she doesn't 'have time for hand-holding'. Henriette wants to convey to Nellie that she doesn't want to have to respond to Nellie's needs *at all*, and that she only respects absolute self-sufficiency. Nellie only hears that her boss is busy and tied up; she doesn't hear the requirement Henriette has placed upon her to act independently at all times and expect a reaction if she doesn't. Nellie's second mistake is that she believes that if she can turn dormant accounts into active fee-earning accounts her manager will be pleased with her. This is sort of true, but not the whole story. Nellie doesn't realize that her manager wants her staff to demonstrate personal loyalty to *her*, and to behave in ways she approves of, as well as to perform consistently well. Of course she wants effective performers – she sets very high standards – but that alone isn't enough. In the end Nellie doesn't win the hotel chain back for the firm, which means, as far as Henriette is concerned, that she has failed *her*. Nellie is now in a vulnerable position vis-à-vis her manager because she has failed to win back a client and doesn't readily conform to Henriette's behavioral expectations of her. With a failed account and an ineffective relationship with her manager – at least from Henriette's point of view – Nellie is likely to get left out in the cold. Nellie's third mistake is that she never seriously considers the possibility that, alien to her though it might be, she could learn how to handle Henriette from Dirkje. She carries on for six months handling her relationship with her boss in her easy-going way, looking to build rapport where none is offered and hoping that her boss will one day see the value of her hard work and committed approach. Henriette isn't impressed by these attributes alone and doesn't come to see Nellie as particularly valuable. In the end she loses patience with Nellie and takes her key account away from her.

- Nellie doesn't manage to win the hotel chain back to the company. What mistakes does she make when relaying this information to her boss?

Nellie qualifies her failure to win the account by citing her hard work on the bid, her long hours, how close the decision was and how she has been dedicated and committed to the project. This is the wrong tack to take with Henriette. Nellie would have been better off telling her manager factually what had happened – that she narrowly failed to get the business – and providing written proof of her claim that it was a close call, if she could. She should then have asked Henriette where this outcome leaves her with regards to her financial targets. Knowing that Henriette wants to double revenues within the next five years, Nellie needs to make a direct link between her failed attempt to bring in business and her boss's targets, in order to convince her boss that she is thinking about her and her position. This might have felt like high-risk to Nellie, but it would have demonstrated Nellie's loyalty to Henriette and could have lessened her anger at Nellie's failure to bring in the business. While not a foolproof plan, this strategy would have given Nellie a better chance of avoiding Henriette's wrath than going to her office expecting support and sympathy for a perceived failure.

- During the team update meeting that Henriette calls, she is cold and cutting with Nellie in front of the whole team. How should Nellie have interpreted this behavior?

Nellie doesn't read Henriette's cold anger toward her at the team meeting as being out-of-proportion to the issues being discussed. It's a team update meeting and there is nothing contentious in it. She interprets her manager's coldness as another of Henriette's irascible moments. It isn't. It is a clear signal that something specific is wrong, and something big enough for Henriette to give Nellie a warning about in public. Had Nellie read this signal correctly, she might have realized that something was brewing. She could then have taken steps either to protect herself, or to go and speak with her manager about what is wrong and what needs to happen to set things on an even keel again. But Nellie does nothing for two days and is completely floored when her manager removes her top account from her and gives it to her colleague Dirkje instead.

■ Henriette removes Nellie's cosmetics account from her and gives it to Dirkje on the pretext of incentivizing top performers. Nellie doesn't react effectively this time either. What could she have done to try and salvage this situation?

Nellie needs to go onto the front foot straightaway and tell her boss, in front of Dirkje, that removing the account from her at this stage of proceedings represents a big risk to the company. She needs to point out, forcibly, that the client has been dealing with her and that, to them, a switch of contacts at this stage would be inexplicable and potentially damaging. Depending on how her boss handles this she might then go on to say that being given dormant clients in her opening portfolio is a challenge she has risen to effectively, and that being undermined now, and being confronted at an earlier team meeting, is not appropriate and needed to be redressed. Nellie needs to remain professional and unemotional, not display any hurt, and deal with the issues presented at the meeting by her boss as if they were business issues at any other meeting. This approach will maintain her credibility in an undermining situation. She needs to address the fact that her account is being given to a peer who has no experience of the client involved and who is fully committed to other work. She also needs to state that she isn't happy with the decision, the way it is being communicated or the implications of it for her career.

Let's now take a look at the political dynamics from Dirkje's viewpoint:

■ Dirkje has learned how to handle Henriette. Given the definition of political behavior introduced in the previous chapter, to what extent is his decision to adopt behavior his boss approves of political tactic on his part?

It isn't a political tactic per se. It is a way of working effectively with a challenging and difficult boss. Dirkje's decision to adopt behavior which keeps his relationship with Henriette workable is not political for two reasons: firstly, it doesn't result in him pursuing his own personal agenda at the expense of his role goals; and secondly, it doesn't gain him power or status or kudos without him being open about it. Everyone in the office can see that Dirkje has learned how to work with Henriette, and can also see that he works just as hard as everyone else. He doesn't benefit from her patronage beyond being given more delegated work than his colleagues. The issue for Dirkje is: to what extent does he realize just how precarious a position he is in. Being Henriette's favorite will not help him if he fails her. She will be just as ruthless with him as with anyone else.

- Dirkje accepts the removal of the cosmetics company from Nellie and its placement with him. To what extent does this represent a betrayal of his relationship with Nellie?

Nellie certainly thinks it is. She could begin to see Dirkje as two-faced: supportive to her face while duplicitous behind her back. However, it is fair to say that Dirkje probably didn't know that Henriette would give him Nellie's client account, and so couldn't warn Nellie about the content of the meeting beforehand. In a split second he has to decide how to react to Henriette's switch of accounts, and he makes the decision which is right for him, the only decision he can make. Only time will tell whether his relationship with Nellie will recover or not. However, Dirkje now has to deliver on the cosmetics account. Having been given this poisoned chalice he will have to win the business for the company or face Henriette's reaction to his failure.

Let's now take a look at the political issues surrounding Henriette's approach to managing Nellie and Dirkje:

- Henriette decides to remove Nellie's cosmetics account from her and give it to Dirkje on the pretext of incentivizing him. What is her real motivation for this maneuver?

Henriette wants to achieve two things simultaneously. Firstly, she wants to punish Nellie for failing her professionally and personally and to demonstrate her power in the group. She uses the term 'incentivizing top performers' as a rouse to make her switch of accounts seem like a sound managerial decision. Secondly, she wants to reward Dirkje for meeting her personal agenda by adopting a style of handling her which she likes and of which she approves.

- Given the definitions of political behavior introduced in the previous chapter, to what extent is Henriette's behavior toward Nellie at this point politically motivated?

Henriette's behavior toward Nellie is highly political. She lets her personal feelings for Nellie dictate the way in which she handles her, and her decision is primarily about flexing her power over her two team members. However, her decision is dangerous for the company which employs her, as Henriette's removal of the cosmetics company from Nellie might just backfire on her. Although she can justify her decision to her seniors by saying that Nellie failed last time and Dirkje always delivers, the client might not be too happy to be passed on to someone new at a late stage of proceedings. Henriette hasn't really considered this, and dismisses it when Nellie brings it up, albeit as a complaint, at the meeting. Having let her personal chagrin with Nellie dominate her decision-making process, she now lets it blind her to the obvious pitfall of switching accounts.

The last question invites you to reflect on how a clearer understanding of her boss's political intent could have helped Nellie from the outset:

■ Nellie could have handled her manager so that, despite failing to win back the hotel chain, she might have continued her work with the cosmetics company. Given the definition of political behavior introduced in the previous chapter, how would a clearer understanding of her boss's political mindedness have helped Nellie handle her more skilfully?

Nellie treats her boss as a pressurized, sometimes angry, sometimes manipulative manager, but sees her as being far less politically minded than she really is. Had Nellie understood the nature of Henriette's political approach she could have handled her boss differently, and might not have had to face the ignominy of losing her top prospective account.

Nellie needs to understand two things, neither of which seems apparent to her. Firstly, she needs to realize that everything her boss does is political. This means that Henriette deliberately uses behavior which primarily reflects her inner agenda, no matter how business-orientated her presentation of these decisions is afterwards. The two most important inner factors that Henriette takes into account when making her decisions are the degree to which a team member succeeds and the degree to which a team member demonstrates personal loyalty to her. Secondly, Nellie also needs to realize that when riled Henriette reacts aggressively. In this mode one of her favorite tactics is to play one colleague off against another. This serves her purpose by undermining the relationship between the two colleagues, leaving one of them out in the cold and therefore powerless, while giving the other her backing and therefore approval.

Had Nellie realized that these two factors are preeminently important to Henriette, she could have used a completely different approach with her manager from early on. It's all in the presentation. Firstly, knowing Henriette respects self-sufficiency, she could have avoided showing any upset, disappointment or emotion to her manager and presented herself as being, at all times, resolute, determined and on top of things. This would have preserved Henriette's respect and made it harder for her to find a reason to demote Nellie. Secondly, knowing that Henriette wants to see evidence of personal loyalty could have enabled Nellie to learn from Dirkje how to manage her boss effectively on a day-to-day basis. This approach would have meant that when Nellie failed to bring in the hotel chain she would have had some political currency in the bank, and might have retained her manager's faith long enough to be given an opportunity to secure the cosmetic firm's business.

This case study has focused on the relationship between two non-political team members and their politically minded manager. It has illustrated the dilemmas and challenges that working for a politically minded boss can create for those working for them, and, indeed, the potential risk that politically minded managers pose to the company that employs them too. It demonstrates that it is possible to work for a politically minded boss, but that to do so effectively you will need to use a specific approach with them from the offset.

Having highlighted these points, we now need to get to grips with how you manage the political behavior you encounter at work everyday. We will start by taking an in-depth look at the different values and styles people use in your workplace, and examining how these differences affect the political dynamics in your key working relationships.

The Politics of Values and Styles

In this chapter we are going to explore in detail the political dynamics created by having people of widely differing values and behavioral styles working together side by side in the workplace; people who may have nothing in common with one another beyond the same employer, but who have to find ways of working productively with one another day in, day out. This chapter will introduce you to the complexities of the different style and value systems that you and your colleagues may use at work, and will explore the political elements these differences create in your workplace.

The aim of the chapter is to clarify the different priorities, perspectives, goals and concerns that you and your colleagues may have, so that you can better manage the interpersonal tensions and conflicts that can be created when you work with people who do things in different ways to you. The chapter will provide you with insight and tools to help you recognize tensions caused by style clashes as opposed to tensions caused by political behavior.

DIFFERENT PRIORITIES, DIFFERENT PERSPECTIVES

Accurately identifying which category a particular tension or conflict belongs to is important in determining how you subsequently handle the difficulties it creates for you. For instance, where a colleagues' behavior isn't politically motivated, and the tensions between you are a result of a genuine values or styles clash, you will need to sit down and decide how to work effectively together, even if, in some particularly tricky circumstances, you require skilled help to enable you to make progress.

But, where your colleagues' behavior is politically motivated, you will need to take a different tack in handling the issues their approach creates for you. It probably won't be possible for you to sit down and simply sort it out. As we've seen, the politically motivated person is, by their very nature, unwilling to use collaborative, open and transparent behavior. Any attempt you make to have a problem-solving conversation with a truly politically minded colleague could ultimately fail, even if, at the time of having of it, you believe you are making progress. Unfortunately, subsequent events are likely to demonstrate to you that, whatever you believe you had agreed with your colleague at the time, they may well leave the meeting and do whatever they consider to be in their best interests, whether or not this happens to coincide with what they said to you previously, or with what you believe they said to you previously.

So let's start by equipping you with the knowledge and tools you'll need to make an accurate diagnosis about whether the underlying cause of a tense and challenging relationship is that you are working with a political colleague or is that you are working with a colleague who uses a different style to you and naturally sees things from a different, perhaps radically different, perspective to you. Let's look at an example to help establish these principles.

Example One: Different Styles, Different Agendas

The manager of a software development firm needs two of his employees to work together on a joint program for a new and potentially important customer. The manager decides to ask two employees who have quite differing styles to work together because he hopes that their different ways of doing things will prove useful for the project. He hopes that the big picture, action-orientated approach of one colleague will be well complimented by the detail orientated, more cautious and planned approach of the other, and that together they'll make a good team. He briefs them together, making it clear to them that the project must be in on time and to the highest quality standards. He anticipates that it will take ten weeks of their joint time to deliver. The manager knows that these two employees haven't worked together on a major piece of work before and are very different animals so, in some sense, he knows he is taking a risk putting them together on such an important piece of work. However, he has faith in their individual and collective skills and is sure that, given the importance of the project, they will work well together for the good of the firm.

After five weeks the two colleagues are making heavy weather of working in tandem. Their relationship is marked by habitual niggling disagreement, interspersed with sporadic conflict. They have different ways of doing things, see most situations from divergent perspectives and value dissimilar things at work. Having expressed their views on an issue, they rarely agree on a way forward and waste a lot of time arguing about the merits of their different perspectives. They both claim to be working toward the same overall project objective, but whenever there is a decision to be made, or a discussion to be had, they present their widely differing views on how to proceed and then argue over the disparities between them. After five weeks of working together, they haven't found an effective way to merge their perspectives constructively and as a result progress is slow.

Their manager forms a view that he can no longer allow them to simply get on with it. He decides that enough is enough and tells the two employees to get in a room and sort out their differences. He tells them not to emerge until they have decided how they are going to work together. After two hours, and no apparent resolution, he intervenes and speaks to each of them in turn in private, asking them what are the key issues, from their perspective, that make it so hard for them to work well together. The first colleague says her more methodical co-worker holds up progress, doesn't make things happen and is jeopardizing the project. When it is his turn to meet with his manager the second colleague says that he thinks his more vigorous colleague disregards practical considerations and risks, and doesn't plan enough. As a result of these discussions the manager decides that the style differences between the two colleagues are such that he needs to act. He reassigns the more cautious of his two colleagues to another project and replaces him on the high-profile project. The manager does this for purely pragmatic reasons: he wants to get the project completed on time, he doesn't believe that the two original colleagues are going to resolve their differences and he doesn't want to waste any more time. He does not realize that in making this move, he has played right into the hands of one of the two colleagues, and alienated the other.

Example One: Analyzing the Political Dynamics

Let's examine what has happened here, starting with the manager. Their manager is not politically motivated in this instance. He wants to bring his project in on time and impress his new customer. He wants to end the waste of time and resources that has resulted from the two colleagues not working effectively together. However, his solution carries a risk; the third colleague will have to get up to speed quickly and, in joining a project part-way through, will have a short space of time to understand what has already been accomplished, what is yet to be done and how to work productively with her new colleague, someone who is likely to see herself as the senior member of the partnership. If the third employee is able to handle these dynamics she could make a valuable contribution to the project, and it may yet come in on time. However, given the agenda of the first colleague, the outcome for her new team member isn't clear at the outset.

Let's now look at the first colleague in more detail, and especially at the issues in her character which her manager seems to have overlooked. She behaves politically throughout this scenario. She uses a style which focuses on the big picture and on generating momentum. In and of itself, this is fine. But she forms an early judgment that her style is superior to her colleague's and she determines to give him a hard time. She does not take pleasure in working with her more thoughtful and careful – or as she sees it – pedantic colleague. She dislikes him, his way of working and his emphasis on planning. She thinks he lacks the basic ability to think on his feet, make a quick decision and be excited and enthused about progress. She has a high need to feel in control, and does not want to work with someone who, as she sees it, prevents progress by planning and evaluating when it isn't necessary. She doesn't want to work closely with him, preferably wants him off the project and doesn't see why she should hide her emotional reaction to him, one of increasing frustration and contempt. She prolongs arguments at every opportunity, pointing out the downside of his approach and the benefits of her own. She doesn't listen to his ideas or seek to take value from them. Her aim in creating and exacerbating disputes between them is not to improve the quality of their decision making and problem solving. It is a reflection of her emotional reaction to her colleague and is driven by her hidden agenda, to take control of the project by getting him re-assigned elsewhere.

Let's now look at the second of the two colleagues, the one who uses a style characterized by a focus on the detail and thorough planning. This colleague is behaving nonpolitically throughout this scenario. But he is much more tenacious than his colleague realizes. While he would like to work with someone less stressful to deal with, he is also committed to his employer and is highly conscientious. He wants to do a good job, and wants the project to be a high quality piece of work. So he gives as good as he gets, argues and counterargues, determined to balance out the maverick streak – as he sees it – in his colleague. A lot of his energy goes into managing his relationship with her, and he comes to over-rely on planning and monitoring progress as a way of checking if the project is on track or not. In some senses he does prevent action, but it is because he wants to make sure that the actions that are taken are the right ones in the right order and to the right standard.

When the manager steps in he does so without paying sufficient attention to the intrapersonal dynamics within each person and focuses instead on the interpersonal issues between them. He fails to understand their individual motivations and doesn't ask the right questions about the underlying causes of their fractious relationship.

He chooses to take their unproductive working relationship at face value, and decides that they are two colleagues who are letting their style and value differences get in the way of them working together as a team. So he takes a view about which of them to replace and acts. It could have gone either way, but he was swayed – and manipulated – by the exasperation of the first colleague who told him, in his private meeting with her, that her colleague was slowing things down and jeopardizing the project. By failing to fully understand her agenda, the manager played right into her hands, even though he thought he was doing his best for the project. He removes the colleague who – for all his methodical, slow style – had the best interests of the project at heart and leaves it in the hands of the colleague who refuses to see beyond her own style preferences.

VALUES AND STYLE DIFFERENCES: THE KEY PRINCIPLE

It is vital to get behind the fact of an interpersonal conflict in order to ascertain whether its cause is:

- Political and nothing at all to do with style differences – even if it is presented as such. This is the approach of the first colleague.
- Nonpolitical and about style differences that the parties haven't found a way to resolve or don't know how to resolve. This is the approach of the second colleague.

In the above example, both colleagues agree on the overall project goal, so their conflicts are not caused by them working to disparate objectives. Nonetheless, their working relationship was unproductive for their employer. Their interpersonal tensions took up valuable time and energy which were needed by the project and which were being paid for by their employer. But they did so for different reasons.

The first colleague acted out of her hidden agenda to unsettle her colleague and eventually get him reassigned. To this end, she deliberately maintained and exacerbated the differences between them and, when she had the opportunity, told her boss that she thought her colleague was a danger to the project. This was a lie. The second colleague wanted to make sure the project was a success, and tried hard to get to grips with his working relationship with his more robust colleague. He was genuinely unable to find a way through their difficulties and challenges and, when given an opportunity to give his side of the story, told the truth as he saw it, that his colleague didn't attend sufficiently to detail. His relationship with his manager suffered as a result of him being removed from the project. Ultimately he was reassigned because he didn't realize that his manager was scared that the project would fail, and that his manager would feel the need to do something – anything – to prevent that situation from happening.

If both of them did actually want to work effectively together but found that, given the significant style and values differences between them, they didn't know how to, this scenario could have ended very differently. In this case the issues between them – purely style differences – could have been resolved through them sitting down and doing the hard work of agreeing processes by which to make decisions and solve problems together, or through the help of their human resources or learning and development colleagues, or a skilled coaching and development professional who could facilitate this conversation.

In order to make an accurate judgment about what underlies a contentious relationship at work – and therefore how to handle its tensions – you need to be able to recognize the different styles people use at work. So let's now examine four different work styles, and the four different sets of values that underpin those styles, in some detail. We will do this using ideas which I have adapted and derived from behavioral styles theory. There are a number of behavioral styles theories and the ideas I present below use some of the concepts presented in Everett T. Robinson (1995). Having outlined the four styles we'll then explore your style preferences, and those of your key colleagues.

FOUR DIFFERENT WORKING STYLES

I firmly believe that the starting point for being able to handle other people well – including how to handle people who are behaving politically – is to know yourself well. So we will start with you and your style and values at work. Below are descriptions of four different working styles. You might naturally use:

- Only one of the styles all the time. In this case you have a clear preference for the values that underpin that style in comparison with any of the other sets of values.
- A blend of two or three of the styles simultaneously. In this case you pay more attention to a specific blend of values in comparison with any other sets of concerns.
- All four styles simultaneously. In this case you set yourself the challenge of findings ways of satisfying four potentially competing sets of concerns all the time.
- Different styles with different groups of workplace contacts. In this case you might, for instance, use one combination of the styles with

your boss, a different combination of styles with your customers, and a different combination of styles again with your peer group or team members.

As you read through the four style descriptions that follow, remember that everyone uses their own style and there are no rights or wrongs about style preference. You might find that you particularly identify with one or more of the styles when things are going well for you and that, when they are going badly for you and you feel under pressure, you identify more with a different style or blend of styles. So, when you consider your usual workplace behavior when things are going well for you which of the following four styles, or which combination of the four styles, do you most identify with? The following descriptions of the four styles are adapted from Chapter 4 of *Starting and Running a Coaching Business* by Aryanne Oade published by How To Books (2009).

Style One: You are goal and objective-orientated, you think factually and logically and you enjoy challenges in your work and private life. You like to take the initiative at work, are action-orientated and prefer to be in charge, if at all possible. When you talk about your work you like to describe the outcomes that your approach will generate. You enjoy generating momentum and like to work within a clear structure. You naturally set and clarify direction for your work and worry if you think you might miss an opportunity. You expect to be rewarded for achieving your goals. You enjoy setting direction for a project or piece of work and get energy from being involved in what's going on around you.

Style One, Summary of Key Values: Those of you who identify, at least to some extent, with the style described above may well find that you:

- Seek out opportunities to direct proceedings and take charge of the work you are involved in.
- Have a penchant for generating momentum and demanding continued productivity, even in pressured situations.
- Naturally clarify direction for the work you are involved in.
- Like to give and receive information in bullet points and headlines.
- Take a strategic view, and speak about outcomes and future-orientated plans.
- Get frustrated if progress is slow; or you perceive that the actions of other people are preventing you from making headway; or if you cannot directly influence factors key to the success of your work.

- Get concerned if you think you are missing an opportunity; or if you are unable to capitalize on the possibilities in a situation.

Remember that you could employ any combination of the styles; you could use just one style all the time, or a blend of two or three, or you could use all four of them simultaneously. With that in mind, whether or not you identify with some or all of the characteristics described above, to what extent do you identify with the characteristics of the following style?

Style Two: You are goal and objective-orientated, and enjoy being self-sufficient and self-reliant. You are also cautious, systematic, planned and thorough in the way you approach your work. You demonstrate your competence by including plenty of detail about what you are proposing, why you are proposing it, and how you see your plans working. You tend not to make errors of fact. It is important to you that you plan in advance of a project to make sure that you think through possible scenarios and anticipate potential problems up front. You want to do high quality, meticulous work. You are at your best when you can work to agreed principles or use logical analysis. Your data-centred approach means that you dislike being asked to move ahead if you haven't had sufficient time to gather and analyze relevant information. In these cases you can struggle to make an effective decision, lacking the data upon which to base your conclusions. You are at your best when you work in a role that gives you genuine independence, and which enables you to give priority to facts and principles.

Style Two, Summary of Key Values: Those of you who identify, at least to some extent, with the style described above may well find that you:

- Seek out opportunities to ensure quality and manage risk in the work you are involved in.
- Have a penchant for planning, monitoring and evaluating progress, a combination which brings a degree of predictability to your work.
- Naturally clarify the fact of the matter, supplying data to support your case.
- Like to speak about the background and rationale, providing detailed supporting data and facts.
- Make a point of asking what can be learned from previous work that could prevent error going forward.
- Get frustrated if you are expected to move ahead without having had time to consider the situation; if you perceive that you have to make a decision without having sufficient data to do so effectively;

or if you do not understand a situation fully enough to take charge of it.

- Get concerned if you think your understanding of a situation is insufficiently thorough; or if you are unable to identify, or plan to overcome, all possible risks.

Style One and Style Two are both primarily goal and objective-orientated styles. Those of you who identify with them, at least in part, will be primarily task-focused in the way in which you approach your work, although the styles emphasize different things as being more or less important. The following two styles are people and process-orientated. It is quite possible for you to use goal-orientated and people-focused styles simultaneously. So, whether or not you identify with either of the styles outline above, to what extent do you identify with the following style?

Style Three: You are people and process oriented and enjoy building relationships characterized by warmth and rapport. You are naturally supportive and enjoy working as part of a team. You would like to carry out work that makes a difference to someone, be it your colleagues, your customers or your manager. You tend to demonstrate a high degree of commitment to your work and, in return, expect active participation from those working with you. You find it stressful if you work without harmony and warmth for long periods of time, or if you work with people who don't seem to want or need your help. You are at your best when you can convey your personal conviction about the best way to approach a piece of work or solve a problem.

Style Three, Summary of Key Values: Those of you who identify, at least to some extent, with the style described above may well find that you:

- Seek out opportunities to be a supportive mentor to the people who work with and for you.
- Have a penchant for assessing the impact of decisions on other people and for maintaining harmony.
- Naturally respond to other people, providing a sense of committed responsibility to the work you undertake.
- Like to work in an environment where people learn from one another, develop new skills and resolve conflicts.
- Are a reliable performer who contributes loyalty and understanding to the workplace.
- Get frustrated if you are expected to work with people who take advantage of your willingness to help others; or who don't involve

you or your colleagues in decisions which affect them; or who don't think about what the decisions will mean to those who have to implement them.

■ Get concerned if you think your work is not appreciated or if your high standards for interpersonal conduct are not met.

Style Four: You are people and process oriented and enjoy having influence with your colleagues and workplace contacts. You have a healthy network of contacts and find it easy to find something to say to most, if not all, of the people you work with. You are naturally adaptable and outgoing. When speaking with a colleague you naturally talk about what the two of you can do for each other and together. You are skilled at influencing people and promoting yourself. You instinctively know how to put an argument across to someone, and may relate the same facts in different ways to different people in different conversations. You are open-minded and often delay making a decision in order to keep your options open. You are comfortable working without much structure and tend to see all sides to an argument. You are often at your best when your role at work involves you bringing people together to achieve a common aim.

Style Four, *Summary of Key Values*: Those of you who identify, at least to some extent, with the style described above may well find that you:

■ Seek out opportunities to facilitate and broker relationships at work in order to have influence and make things happen.

■ Have a penchant for remaining flexible, managing other people's perceptions and marketing your achievements.

■ Naturally like to experiment, and enjoy using your resourcefulness to get round problems and obstacles.

■ Like to be in the spotlight, acquiring influential contacts at work.

■ Are sociable, get on well with many people and enjoy working as part of a team.

■ Get frustrated if you are expected to work in a highly structured environment with tight deadlines; or with people who keep their heads down and get on with their work; or with unfriendly, critical colleagues.

■ Get concerned if credit which you think is owing to you is given to other people; if your work keeps you away from influential colleagues; or if your work means that you spend all day on your own away from other people.

It is beyond the scope of this book to describe all the complexities of behavioral styles theory in detail, and there is much more to say about it. I use it in my work because it provides an effective language for discussing why some colleagues have a hard time working together, and what to do to enable them to establish a more productive relationship. For our purposes you need to have some idea about your own style preferences, and to be able to recognize other people's styles as well, so that we can explore the tensions and conflicts that might arise for you in the workplace. If you'd like to make a detailed exploration into style at work the Recommended Reading List at the back of the book will point you in the right direction.

EXPLORING YOUR STYLE

Having read through the style descriptions above, you may now like to read them through again with the following questions in mind. Knowing your own style preferences, and being able to recognize the different but equally valid preferences of other people, is important for how you decide to handle some political dynamics at work. So it might be worth your while to revisit the descriptions above and jot down your answers to each of the following questions in the space below it:

- Which style, or which combination of styles, do you use when things are going well for you at work and you are at your best?

- Which characteristics of this style or styles do you value, and in what way are they useful to you in your work?

- Which characteristics of this style or styles do other people dislike or find challenging to deal with? What, if anything, can you do about this?

- Which style, or which combination of styles, do you use when things are not going well for you at work and you are under pressure?

> [blank box]

- Which characteristics of this style or styles do you value, and in what ways are they valuable to you when you are under pressure?

> [blank box]

- Which characteristics of this style or styles do other people experience as challenging?

> [blank box]

READING YOUR COLLEAGUE'S STYLES

You've already identified which style, or combination of styles, you use at work. You've also determined how your natural style might change under pressure. You might now like to consider the styles your key colleagues use at work. So let's focus on how you might recognize these styles, before examining an example of the political elements created when two people of different styles, and unequal organizational influence, work together.

The following descriptions illustrate the four different styles, or combinations of styles, that your colleagues might favor. As you read through them, you might want to keep in mind a key colleague with whom you work on a regular basis. The following descriptions of four potential colleagues' styles are adapted from Chapter 4 of *Starting and Running a Coaching Business* by Aryanne Oade published by How To Books (2009).

Does Your Colleague Use Style One? Your colleague wants to hear headline information, consistently presented, and will be most interested in what can be achieved, by when and how. She is quick to make up her mind and, once convinced, is unlikely to be easily swayed. She is primarily objective-orientated, and likes a straightforward factual discussion. She would like to focus the debate on what your proposals will do for her, and what those results will mean to her. She likes working within a clear structure and probably values self-sufficiency and independence. She sets high targets for herself, and will be interested in how your proposals will challenge or stretch her. She might become impatient with detail, but will want to hear about the big picture concepts behind your proposals. She may ask you for specific information from time to time, but is more likely to want to concentrate on what you are proposing, what it will achieve and how these outcomes will benefit her and her plans.

Does Your Colleague Use Style Two? Your colleague likes to think through, in some detail, the implications of anything new. He is likely to be practical, goal-oriented, rational and cautious when he is first confronted with a new set of proposals. He would like to hear a systematic presentation of your ideas, in as much detail as you can manage. He might want a written summary of your proposals as well as a verbal discussion of them, so that he can go away and think things through before returning to you with further questions or for more input. He is likely to want to reflect on what you've said before making a firm decision. He is precise and orderly and will expect full answers to any questions or issues he raises with you. Being quite risk-averse, at least until he's had time to think, your colleague will respond well to an approach that emphasizes how your proposals tie into his current way of doing things. He is data-centred and likely to be knowledgeable about his areas of expertise. You can expect him to question you closely about your knowledge of your subject areas.

Does Your Colleague Use Style Three? Your colleague is interested in people, values relationships and teamwork, and enjoys being in mutually supportive workplace. He is probably quite warm interpersonally, and will respond favorably to a collaborative way of working. Your ability to influence him may be connected to your ability to demonstrate your interpersonal skills such as listening, building rapport and trust, or being able to provide kind challenges. Your colleague will appreciate being asked to input to key decision-making and problem-solving discussions. He'd like to be consulted, included and asked for his views, especially about issues which affect the people and teams he works with. Describing the interpersonal values behind your proposals, and how they will enhance team work or improve the quality of service offered to clients, will serve you best when trying to influence him; as will being able to demonstrate to him that you have thought about the impact of your proposals on the people who will implement them and be affected by them.

Does Your Colleague Use Style Four? Your colleague sees herself as an able networker, someone who is influential and well connected at work. She is probably skilled with people and a shrewd judge of character. She will enjoy working in an unstructured process, one that leaves room for evolving plans and changes of direction. She may be willing to plan up front, but, having developed that plan, may well only refer to it occasionally from then on. Her natural style involves being spontaneous and open to new developments, and she is adept at taking things in her stride. When you are trying to influence her it would serve you best to focus the conversation on what you and she can accomplish together. You might like to clarify the ways in which your proposals will result in her gaining access to more influential people in the workplace, or will enable her to raise her profile at work. This colleague wants to enjoy her workplace relationships, and would like to be popular and admired. She'd like you to enjoy working with her as much as she'd like to enjoy working with you, so be prepared for an informal chat before getting down to work.

EXPLORING YOUR COLLEAGUES' STYLES

You might like to spend a few minutes thinking about the styles used by colleagues with whom you have effective and ineffective working relationships. You can jot down your answers to the following questions in the space below each one:

- Identify a colleague with whom you have an effective working relationship. Which of the four styles, or which combination of the four styles, do you think your colleague uses when things are going well for them, and how does this shift when they are under pressure?

- Which characteristics of his or her styles do you value, and why are these characteristics important to you in your work?

■ Identify a colleague with whom you have an ineffective working relationship. Which of the four styles, or which combination of the four styles, do you think your colleague uses when things are going well for them, and how does this shift when they are under pressure?

■ Which characteristics of his or her style do you find challenging, and why are these characteristics problematic for you to deal with in your work?

■ What conclusions have you come to about how to better manage your relationship with this colleague going forward?

Having examined both your style and the styles used by some of your colleagues, let's now consider a second example which focuses on the dynamics of style clashes in detail. It explores the challenges faced by a relationship-orientated number two reporting to a newly appointed goal-orientated manager.

Example Two: Style Clash or Political Behavior?

A large pizza chain hires a new Finance Manager, poaching him from their main rival. The new Finance Manager wants to employ his long-standing number two from his previous role to work alongside him at his new place of work. He is prevented from doing so by his new boss who wants him to work with the existing number two in the Finance Department, an effective and well-liked man who has been with the restaurant chain for over 10 years. Disappointed, the new Finance Manager agrees to do so. On arriving for his first day at work, the Finance Manager makes a point of telling his boss and his new number two that he hopes he will establish productive and effective working relationships with both of them.

The Finance Manager uses a style which is characterized by a strong emphasis on achieving goals in a methodical, high-quality way. He uses a combination of the first and second styles outlined above, both of which are goal orientated; but, if pushed, he has a slight preference for the analytical, second style over the action-orientated, first style. The Finance Manager places great emphasis on a detailed, impartial analysis of the facts and is highly logical and linear in the way he thinks and looks at things at work. He is task focused, tends only to speak if it is to progress a piece of work, is quite driven in his approach and is a cool, but not unfriendly, character.

The incumbent number two uses the first, third and fourth styles outlined above in equal measures. He wants to achieve his goals effectively and efficiently, but he also places weight on building rapport with his colleagues. He enjoys being around people in the office and, having worked there for 10 years or more, has an extensive informal network of contacts in the department, as well as a number of workplace friends among his colleagues. He wants to build an influential and valued relationship with his new boss, and to be an effective member of his team. He quickly recognizes that their styles are quite different. He characterizes his new manager's style as being about generating momentum while also achieving error-free and high quality outcomes. He characterizes his own style as being about establishing effective, high quality relationships which enable work to be carried out – and goals achieved – productively.

After three months, the two of them have reached stalemate. They don't fall out, they don't argue. But when they work together the number two feels uncomfortable with the stilted and awkward dialog between them. There are many ways in which the number two could respond to this situation. Let's explore three of them:

■ The number two thinks his contribution isn't valued or even necessarily understood by the Finance Manager, and he doesn't enjoy his job any more. He worries that his boss is being deliberately awkward with him, and doesn't really want the relationship to work, even though he said he did on his first day at work. The number two has started to think that his boss is deliberately devaluing his input, and is purposefully trying to make it uncomfortable for him, either to punish him for not being his former number two, or because he hopes to unsettle him enough that he will leave of his own accord so he can hire his former colleague. He is not normally given to a suspicious turn of mind, but then he has never had his verbal input repeatedly treated as frivolous and irrelevant before. He can't really believe that the Finance Manager doesn't understand what he says on a regular basis, but it feels like that to him. When he speaks to his boss, making his characteristic intuitive observations, the Finance Manager looks quite blank, pauses and then bends again to his desk, sometimes without saying anything back. It is as if his remarks have no significance to him. He finds him sober and serious, and actually quite dull to work for. He is aware that if he left to go to another role, his boss would be able to bring in his former number two to do his job in his stead.

- The number two decides that he has had enough of having his input ignored by his manager, and decides to get his own back. He starts to do just what is required in his role, and no more. He is never rude, surly or offhand to his manager, but equally, he doesn't look for opportunities to add value to his work for him either. He puts his energy into other areas of his life, his out-of-work social activities and his weekend garden design course. The colleagues who have worked with him for a number of years notice the change in him and ask him if he is ok. He deflects their questions. His manager also notices that he seems different but doesn't connect the changes he detects with his own attitude to his number two, doesn't know how to bring the subject up, and leaves it unaddressed. The number two never underperforms badly enough that the issue would become a topic of conversation at his appraisal; but, slowly and surely, he comes to regard his work as a means to an end, rather than giving it pride of place in his life, as he used to do. He enjoys his life outside work much more and is happier overall.

- The number two decides to change tack with the Finance Manager. He, for the moment at least, decides to take him at face value, and therefore to accept that he does want to establish an effective and productive working relationship with him. He starts to speak to him only in business-focused terms, and stops trying to chat informally to him when they work together or meet in the office. He isn't rude or cold, just less communal. He provides him with more background information and factual analysis prior to saying what he wants to say, and no longer assumes that his boss will follow his intuitive leaps of thought. He respects that they do things in different ways and that what might seem to him a chatty, rapport-building comment could come across to his boss as left field and inane. He works hard at adapting his style enough that he and his manager can work together without the awkward silences that used to follow his spontaneous remarks. He decides that he will chat and be informal with other people in the office, and not expect his manager to take part in these types of discussions. He keeps his contact with him professional, business-like and crisp at all times.

Example Two: Analyzing the Political Dynamics

Let's take look at what is happening in these three scenarios starting with the first one:

The First Instance: The number two in this scenario thinks that the Finance Manager's behavior toward him is politically motivated in this instance and that his boss:

- Wants to work with his former number two, and not with him.
- Said that he wanted to establish a productive working relationship with him to make it look good.
- Is trying to engineer a situation in which he feels uncomfortable enough that he decides to leave.
- Purposefully fails to respond to his observations and comments to undermine him.
- Treats his comments and verbal input as frivolous and worthless to reduce his self-esteem.
- Hopes he will move on, leaving the way open for his boss to hire his previous number two.

It is a painful time for the number two. His manager's behavior is not obviously aggressive, unkind or unpleasant. It is however subtly undermining of him and denigrating toward him – or so he thinks. He could be coming to the wrong conclusion in thinking that his boss is acting politically, but he can't know for sure one way or the other. If he does decide to leave he may find a job he enjoys much more – but then again he might find one which is no better or actually worse than his current one.

The Second Instance: The number two doesn't form a view about whether or not the Finance Manager is behaving politically, but responds with a political strategy of his own instead. He decides, whatever his boss's motives, to redress the balance between them by putting less effort and less commitment into his work. He thinks he is justified in taking this course of action because of his manager's attitude to him; he forms the view that his manager doesn't value him, so he won't value his job as much or try as hard as he used to. He:

- Transfers his attention and passion away from work and into his private life.
- Does just enough to get by at work.

- Makes sure that he doesn't overlook anything important, mess up or otherwise behave in a way which would make his conduct a performance issue.
- Feels vindicated at taking this political stance because he is fed up with his manager's reactions to him.

It is an unsettling time for him because those colleagues who know him well recognize that something is up, and ask him about it. He doesn't want to lie, and he doesn't want to come clean either, so he gives vague replies and feels uncomfortable that he isn't being straight with people he's worked with for a long time. He runs the risk of losing some of the positive regard he has built up at the company by doing less than his best, but he has more energy and commitment to give to his life outside work which he subsequently values more.

The Third Instance: The number two thinks that the Finance Manager is acting nonpolitically and that their widely differing styles, values and ways of speaking, acting and thinking at work are behind their awkward working relationship. He decides that his manager is being straight with him when he says he wants their relationship to work, and therefore determines that, at least for the time being, he will:

- Change his behavior with him, recognizing that he is highly goal oriented and prefers to communicate in factual, linear terms.
- Set the context for the points he wants to make to his manager by providing him with data, facts and analysis beforehand.
- Stop assuming that his manager will be able to make intuitive leaps, follow his train of thought spontaneously or want to have informal, chatty contact with him around the office.
- Respect the fact that he is his boss, and get on with the task of adapting to his style enough to makes things smoother between them.

It is a challenging time for him, and he does not know whether or not this strategy will work. But he determines to have a go. He has a good chance of improving the quality of communication he has with his boss, but he has also taken on the hard work of adapting his own style quite significantly to do so.

WHAT WOULD YOU DO?

There is no right or wrong way to handle a situation such as the one the number two finds himself in when his new boss starts at the firm, and there are many other ways in which he could have responded to this situation in addition to the three options outlined above. In the number two's shoes what would you do? You might like to consider this question and jot down your answers to it in the space below:

```



```

THE POLITICAL DYNAMICS SURROUNDING YOUR STYLE

We have seen in this chapter that the same behavior can be interpreted in different ways, and what looks like a well-intentioned motivation can actually be a politically motivated strategy. At the end of the day, how you handle the situations and relationships you find yourself in at work is down to your:

- Reading of the intrapersonal and interpersonal dynamics in a given situation.
- Understanding of what the people in the situation are trying to achieve.
- People-handling and influencing skills.
- Commitment to maintaining quality relationships at work even when it's tough to keep communication channels open.
- Clarity about your own preferred outcome in the situation.

You might like to spend a few minutes thinking about the political dynamics surrounding style differences in your work. You can jot down your answers to the following questions in the space below each one – and you may want to refer back to the answers you gave to previous questions in this chapter as you consider the next set:

- Identify an instance in which you observed a colleague of yours exploiting style differences for political ends. What did they do and why do you think they acted like this?

[ ]

- What impact did this instance have on your working relationship with that colleague?

[ ]

- Identify an instance in which you might have exploited style differences for political ends. What did you do and why did you handle things in this way?

[ ]

- What impact did your tactics have on the situation and your relationships with the people involved in it?

[ ]

- If you were to be in the same situation again tomorrow what, if anything, would you do differently?

[ ]

SUMMARY AND THE NEXT CHAPTER

This chapter has focused on:

- Helping you discern the difference between tensions at work caused by values clashes and tensions at work caused by political behavior.

- Examining the issues that can arise when people with different styles and values are asked to work together, and don't successfully work through their values differences.
- Exploring an example, featuring two people working unproductively together in a software development firm, illustrating how the behavior of one of the characters could be misconstrued by his manager as well intentioned, when it is actually an example of politically motivated strategy.
- Identifying four different working styles with their associated values, characteristics and behavioral traits.
- Examining which style or styles you use when you are at your best, and which you use when things are not going well for you.
- Identifying how to read your colleagues' styles so that you can better understand how to influence and work with them.
- Exploring an example, set in the Finance Department of a large pizza chain, which illustrates what can happen when a manager and his number two use different styles and speak different languages when they work together.
- Examining your experiences of the political dynamics surrounding style differences at work.

The next chapter introduces the second of the six major case studies in the book. Building on the themes of this chapter, the case study illustrates how an important working relationship breaks down because of the unmanaged style differences between the two colleagues – and the political agenda of one of them.

Internal Conflict

BACKGROUND AND CHARACTERS

This case study is set in a bespoke dressmaking business in Boston, Massachusetts, USA. The business is owned by Matthew, who has run it single-handed for eight years. His office and cutting room are behind his shop, which he keeps open while he works, breaking off to serve any customers who walk in from the street. He enjoys a small walk-in trade selling fashion accessories, hats and a few dresses, but makes his main living from working with a number of long-term clients, mainly large department stores and smaller boutiques in Boston, as well as further afield in Washington DC, New York and New Jersey. Ideally he would like to be able to secure more long-term US business beyond the East Coast region.

Each dress he makes is custom-made and he needs to sell 2–3 dresses per month to break even. Matthew's business philosophy is simple. He enjoys what he does, is skilled at it, makes a good living, and works alone out of choice. Being an able salesman and creator of dresses, Matthew does not need a colleague and does not want the responsibilities of being an employer. He keeps his costs low, but is frustrated that he cannot open his shop when he is on a business trip. He enjoys significant customer loyalty and repeat business from the long-term clients who like his brand, his dresses and his style of service.

Ideally, he would like to share some of the day-to-day responsibilities of running the business – especially the constant need to sell and market his products and services – with someone else. He finds his regular sales trips tiring but doesn't see how he can share the sales side of his work with anyone else because he doesn't want to employ anyone. Nonetheless, he worries that, without some additional help, he might find it difficult to find sufficient new clients in the long term to keep his business buoyant.

Brigitte recently moved to Boston from Dallas. She is a buyer for the wholesale retail trade, and highly successful at her job. Two months after her relocation, however, her employer merged with another company and, despite her excellent record, Brigitte's role was made redundant. Brigitte has a six-month nonnegotiable lease on her rented apartment in Boston, so she decides to stay on in the city and look for alternative employment. She is aware that she might have to switch industries. She meets Matthew at a mutual friend's dinner party, likes the sound of his business and his values, and asks him for a job. Matthew explains that he doesn't have roles for other people in his business and changes the subject.

Brigitte doesn't take no for an answer. She likes the idea of working in a small business with one other person, and doing something creative and novel like dressmaking. Although she has no experience of dress design or production, she does know about the retail trade and believes that she will quickly learn about custom-made dress manufacture. She is confident in her own abilities, practical and bright, so she approaches Matthew again. She receives the same response that Matthew doesn't want to become an employer.

Over the next few weeks Brigitte visits Matthew's shop several times. She explains that her previous role has gained her high-quality contacts in the retail trade across the mid-West, many of whom she has worked with for years, and she is sure that she can introduce Matthew to new markets and clients. She suggests that Matthew take her on and promises that, if she is unsuccessful in creating new business for him, or at learning the skills of dressmaking, she will pay Matthew back whatever she owes him in salary. She tells Matthew that she has never failed at anything in her life and isn't about to start now.

Matthew is impressed by her tenacity and self-belief. He likes her and thinks she had a tough break losing her job so soon after relocating. He believes her when she says she has high-quality retail contacts in the mid-West. He has some misgivings about whether she realizes how steep the learning curve will be, but is comforted that she has promised to repay him if their plans don't work out. He changes his mind and decides to give her a chance. He hires Brigitte on a one-year contract, with a one-month termination clause either way. This is a big step for him and one which means that he, as well as Brigitte, will need to learn to work in different ways. He is hopeful that hiring Brigitte will mean that he gains new business in the mid-West, and that she will bring the practical support and contacts he needs to take his business forward.

THE STYLE ISSUES

Matthew uses a mixture of all four behavioral styles simultaneously. Ideally, he wants to:

- Generate momentum on each new commission, design his dresses effectively and efficiently and take advantage of any and all opportunities to sell and market his business.
- Provide a bespoke, high quality, error free service to each and every client.
- Build harmonious and enjoyable relationships with his clients, providing them with a valued and trusted service.
- Maintain an influential network of business contacts.
- Enjoy the process of working with his new colleague, helping her to develop and learn the skills she needs to acquire to become a successful and valued member of his business.

Matthew works very hard and maintaining the high standards he sets for himself is wearing for him. He often feels tired and unsupported. His style doesn't change under pressure; he simply keeps working until he has finished what he is doing, no matter how long it takes him.

When things are going well for her Brigitte's natural style is wholly goal-oriented, and is a combination of the first and second styles. In her new role she sets herself the joint goals of:

- Learning the ins and outs of bespoke dress design and production.
- Selling and marketing Matthew's business to her mid-West contacts.
- Learning how to manage a client account and build high-quality relationships with clients.
- Remaining productive and effective, even when she is under pressure to perform or meet a deadline.
- Becoming a valued and indispensable part of Matthew's business, someone who doesn't make errors and who does add value.

While Matthew knows that Brigitte is primarily goal-focused in her style, what he doesn't realize is that under pressure Brigitte becomes risk averse and very cautious. She steps back from what she is doing and spends time analyzing what is going on, but finds it difficult to make a decision. In this mode she uses the second style only, but because she is afraid to make a mistake, she over-analyzes and quickly gets stuck. She stalls and frequently fails to make any progress toward her goals at all. In this mode she dislikes asking for help. She tries – often unsuccessfully – to work it out for herself, but wastes valuable time and doesn't ask for input. If anyone offers to help her during these deliberations she quite often refuses their offer even when she needs the advice, direction and time they are willing to give her.

THE FIRST QUARTER: APRIL TO JUNE

During their first three months of working together things go very well for the new colleagues. Matthew is delighted to have proactive support in his business. He trusts Brigitte and feels that his office and shop are in good hands. Employing her means that he can keep his shop open even when he is on a business trip, and this reflects favorably in his monthly sales figures for the quarter. Brigitte is delighted, and thinks that the increased sales are a clear reflection of her worth to the business.

Brigitte is quick to identify things she can do to improve the office processes, and is good with the customers who come into the shop. She picks up on the practicalities of dress design and production straight away, talking sensibly with Matthew about how he goes about creating bespoke dresses. Her natural gift for critiquing processes enables her to suggest a number of improvements to the way in which Matthew contracts with his clients and runs his business. Brigitte seems interested and fully engaged with the challenge of learning how to design and make dresses, and seems to enjoy working with Matthew.

Matthew has high expectations of his new employee. He fully expects her to deliver on her promise of taking his business into new markets. The two colleagues talk extensively about how to approach the contacts Brigitte has in mind and what roles each of them will take at forthcoming sales meetings.

Brigitte sends e-mails to all of her key mid-West contacts informing them about her new role. Her e-mails are upbeat and positive, describing the quality and range of Matthew's dresses. She is somewhat surprised, and more than a little deflated, when she doesn't receive any replies.

THE SECOND QUARTER: JULY TO SEPTEMBER

Brigitte starts to get cold feet. For perhaps the first time in her working life she privately asks herself if she hasn't bitten off more than she can chew. She doesn't feel as confident as she did when she got the job. She is worried that her mid-West sales contacts are not going to be interested in Matthew's business or her new role in it, and that perhaps, after all, they won't be keen to do business with her or her new employer. Being terrified of failure she finds this thought so frightening that she buries it deep in her mind almost as soon as she's thought of it. Instead, she determines that Matthew should see her as valuable to his business whether or not she succeeds in bringing in new business and so, heartened by the increased sales revenue for the first quarter of her employment, she suggests that Matthew should hand over the management of his shop to her, so he can concentrate on selling his business and designing and producing dresses.

Matthew is surprised by this suggestion. Up until now he has seen Brigitte as a confident, able and independent employee, someone who seeks out and thrives on new challenges. After all *she* approached *him* for this job, and convinced him that she would do what it takes to learn the ropes. Her suggestion that she manage his shop is at odds with his view of her. He says he needs to think about it. He is well aware that Brigitte has taken on a significant learning curve, and he is also aware that there is only one person in the business from whom to learn and that is him. Since he is so often busy either selling or designing and producing dresses he doesn't have as much time as he'd like to devote to coaching her in any of these activities. He is a conscientious employer. So he suggests to her that she might like to go on a dressmaking course for which he will pay. He is amazed and perplexed when she turns him down, claiming that she wants to learn more before she takes that step. He presses her for an explanation of what she means and she says she is actively learning about fabrics, designs and patterns from the many books he has lent her. In time, she says, she will be ready to go on the course.

Matthew ruefully accepts the logic of this, and certainly doesn't want to pay for Brigitte to go on a course that is scheduled before she is ready to take full advantage of it. He still assumes that she wants to learn the business, and decides that her development needs to be better managed and planned. As a first step he suggests that she travel with him to his next sales meeting. It is in Washington and is scheduled for the following week. He tells her it will be good experience for her and enable her to get a taste of the selling side of his business.

Brigitte doesn't want to go, but does want to maintain her positive relationship with Matthew. She tells him that she'd feel a fraud in the meeting and that, lacking a real role in the dressmaking side of the business, she'd rather wait until she had something to contribute to the conversation. Once more, Matthew is taken aback. He says that he will introduce her as his new employee who is learning the ropes, and that it will be understood that she doesn't have to take an active part in the meeting. She will be there to learn, and can simply listen while remaining silent. Once more Brigitte objects, claiming that it wouldn't be worth the expense of her airfare and hotel bill. She says that she'd be better employed opening the shop and selling stock to walk-in customers.

Matthew is torn. On the one hand he can see quite clearly that Brigitte seems frightened to face her fears about selling and meeting his clients, and wants to remain in the relative safety of the shop. On the other hand, he doesn't want to impose his will on her and order her to go with him; it's not his style. He'd much rather do things through consensus and agreement, and he doesn't want to force Brigitte into a situation where they have a row. He hates conflict, and is highly motivated to avoid using his precious energy locking horns with his only employee. However, he hired Brigitte to sell and market his business to new clients – something he needed help with – and, ultimately, to design and produce dresses. He did not hire her to manage his shop which is something he has done quite effectively for eight years, and doesn't need help with. He decides that he will have to speak seriously with her on his return from the DC trip, and arranges an informal meeting over cake and coffee for the start of October.

Matthew returns from his successful DC business trip with orders for three dresses. In his absence Brigitte has reorganized the shop, improving its layout and window displays. She has also taken orders for six new dresses from one of Matthew's New York department store clients and has sold a small quantity of stock to walk-in customers. She is both upbeat and excited about her two days in sole charge of the shop. Matthew is pleased with the shop redesign, new orders and sales. With his DC orders the business will be busy for the next three to four months.

However, he isn't as upbeat as Brigitte about the overall situation. He is tired, not just from his trip, but from the growing issue of his employee, who is not turning out as he had hoped. He thinks that hiring Brigitte is turning into an expensive mistake. She isn't creating any new business for him. She won't take any risks, she won't try anything new and she isn't doing the job he hired her to do. She is useful in the shop and good with walk-in customers but, as she isn't contributing to her own salary through generating sales, he now has to find her income as well as his own every month. He is starting to see her as an additional overhead he hadn't bargained for and doesn't want. Furthermore, she seems quite content to let him find her salary, and she doesn't seem to realize what an awkward position she has put him in. She seems to think that as long as the business is doing well – which it is – Matthew can have no complaints.

Matthew decides that enough is enough, and plans what he will say at the forthcoming informal meeting he has arranged with Brigitte. He intends to address all these issues with her and refocus her on the real job he hired her to do, generating income.

THE THIRD QUARTER: OCTOBER TO DECEMBER

The informal meeting between Matthew and Brigitte leaves Matthew highly frustrated. He explains to Brigitte that he is aware that she has a lot to learn, that the learning curve is steep and that she only has one person from whom to learn. He says that if his business was bigger, and employed a number of dress designers and producers, she would be able to learn different things from different people at different times, and it would be easier for her. But, as it is, there is only him, and as he is so often tied up with work, he does not have the time or space to help her learn. He says that these issues weigh heavily on his shoulders and that he'd like to work with her to find a way through them.

Throughout this part of the meeting Brigitte sits still, maintaining level eye contact with Matthew. She seems ill at ease, unusually quiet and slightly surly with him. When he asks her what she suggests would be a workable way forward, she remains silent, shifting uncomfortably in her chair, and becomes flushed in the face. She breaks eye contact with Matthew and moves her chair slightly in protest at his line of questioning. Matthew gets the message. She doesn't want to talk about her failure to sell or market. She doesn't want to talk about the learning curve. She wants to stick her head in the sand, and wants Matthew to be quiet so she can go back to her safe place, the shop. Matthew doesn't know what to do for the best. With the nine dresses on order, and his plans for an Open House in the shop at the end of February, he could always use Brigitte to manage the shop day to day. But, and he comes back to this time and again in his mind, she is on the salary of a saleswoman which is much more than he's willing to pay for someone to manage his shop, and he is having to find her entire salary every month in addition to his own.

He decides that he must press on and bring up this key issue with Brigitte at the meeting. But when he does, he is baffled by her sudden anger. She says she is working hard, has managed the shop effectively, has improved its layout and has developed his business processes. She seems hurt as well as angry at his intimation that he is uncomfortable paying her as highly as he is doing to perform these tasks. Matthew tells her that he is the only one generating income, that the deal was that she would be joining him in this activity and that he is uncomfortable that she is not doing so. He tells her he is concerned that she is not progressing as she and he would have liked, and that he is worried that he isn't doing enough to help her develop. But, he tells her, above and beyond all that, he would like her to start to do the job for which he employed her. He is pleased at his firm, supportive tone which, he hopes, conveys to her that he still thinks she can make the grade.

Brigitte thinks for a while and then says that she is not surprised that it is taking a long time. That is all she says. She does not speak again about these issues in the meeting, does not raise any issues with Matthew or ask any questions of him. She seems content to keep her head down and get the meeting over with. Not knowing what else to say, Matthew changes the subject and describes his plans for the Open House he wants to hold in the middle of February. This will be a high-profile event to which he will invite ten selected clients, to pick their brains about the new designs and lines they would like to see him produce and for him to float past them some new ideas about dresses and fabrics he might use in his summer collections. Cleverly, Brigitte suggests that she handle aspects of the event for him. She suggests that, since he is so busy, she could take the logistics off him: things such as the invitations, the layout of the shop, what food will be served and client travel and accommodation arrangements. She tells him that he would have more time to devote to planning the actual event itself if he didn't have to think about these aspects as well. Once more, Brigitte manages to deflect Matthew sufficiently from his agenda, by offering useful help and doing it in a charming and proactive way. The meeting ends with Brigitte enthusing about her new project and with nothing resolved for Matthew at all.

For the next few weeks Matthew is fully stretched meeting orders. Brigitte works in the shop everyday and sometimes comes to him with a suggestion or a new idea for the Open House. They are usually sound ideas, but none of this makes up for the fact that, no matter how competently she manages the shop or handles the Open House arrangements, Matthew does not value these activities. These activities do not compare in his mind with the value Brigitte would have brought to his business by finding new sales contacts. She starts to look less perky, less bright and her confidence sags further. She gets a niggling cold and can't shake it off. She talks of going on a holiday but doesn't ask for time off or arrange anything.

Matthew seems not to want to engage with the issues surrounding Brigitte's role anymore. He finally accepts that she isn't going to join him in generating income for the business and that he will have to continue to find her salary as well as his own for as long as he employs her. He doesn't speak with her again about his disappointment that she hasn't generated sales for his business. He considers the idea of reducing her pay to bring it in line with what he'd be comfortable paying someone to manage his shop. But he can see how lacking in confidence she already is, and doesn't want to take actions which might result in her self esteem reducing any further. So he dismisses the idea.

THE FOURTH QUARTER: JANUARY TO MARCH

The plans for the Open House are well underway. Matthew is excited and nervous about the event, knowing that, when his current orders are fulfilled, he has no further work lined up. Brigitte works diligently at the arrangements for the Open House and, as they get closer to the event itself, starts to worry about her role: what will she do on the day? how will she present herself? what will Matthew's out-of-town clients think of her? She shares some of these concerns with Matthew who is mystified at her questions.

Matthew is working ten hours a day in the lead up to the Open House. His discomfort with Brigitte's role has turned to a mixture of feeling very let down and feeling concerned for her as a person. She is a shadow of the confident and direct woman who persuaded him to give her a job. Her anxieties about her role at the Open House seem to him a reflection of her dip in morale, and he is worried that she won't relate well to his more high-profile department store and boutique clients who attend the event.

The day of the Open House dawns and Brigitte seems very ill at ease waiting for clients to arrive. Matthew greets them and is on top form. The day goes very well, leads to a number of genuine sales opportunities and ends with a key client asking Matthew to join him for a meeting over dinner to discuss his requirements for his summer collection. Brigitte is not invited and takes this as a personal slight. Throughout the day she takes a back seat and doesn't engage clients in conversation. She seems uncomfortable and disappears into the cutting room a number of times. On two occasions she is offhand with clients while offering them refreshments, and Matthew forms the impression that she is distinctly out of place among his more prestigious customers.

The following day she arrives late for work, leaves early and hardly speaks to Matthew. He forms the impression she is sulking. Over the next three weeks, their relationship deteriorates still further. Brigitte becomes churlish and difficult to deal with, and, while carrying out her duties in the shop well enough, is disrespectful and discourteous to her employer. With one month left on her contract Matthew informs her that he will not be renewing her employment into a second year. He tells her that he is going to go back to working on his own, which for him is less stressful and less costly. Brigitte turns on him, telling him he is being arbitrary and foolish. She says that anyone who takes on a new employee has to give it time to work, that he hasn't given her enough time and that he is acting hastily and subjectively in sacking her.

He tells her that it hasn't worked out the way he expected and has cost him a lot of money. Rather than making more profit during the past 12 months, as he hoped, he has worked very hard and has made a small loss due to the unexpected overhead of her salary. He tells her that all the risk has been with him and that he won't employ her for another period of time because he doesn't have any faith that she will make the grade as a saleswoman. She retorts that she just needs time before busting out with the comment, 'I'm not paying you back!' Matthew tells her again that he will not be renewing her contract and, one month later, she leaves the shop for the last time.

ANALYZING THE POLITICAL DYNAMICS: YOUR ROLE

Consider the following questions. They are designed to help you look behind the facts of the case study and examine the political dynamics at play between Matthew and Brigitte. You can jot down your answers to each question in the space below it. The first set of questions invite you to analyze the political dynamics from Brigitte's viewpoint:

- Brigitte operates out of a number of hidden agendas during the year. What are they?

- Throughout her year's employment with Matthew, Brigitte makes a number of political misjudgments. What are her most significant miscalculations?

- Brigitte does actually want to continue to work with Matthew beyond the first year of her employment. What could she have done to preserve her working relationship with him beyond 12 months?

>

- Brigitte struggles with an internal conflict through the latter part of her employment with Matthew. What is the nature of her internal conflict?

>

The next set of questions invites you to analyze the political dynamics from Matthew's viewpoint:

- When he offers her a job, Matthew takes Brigitte's claims about herself at face value. What are his biggest miscalculations about her?

>

- Matthew makes a number of errors of judgment as a manager throughout the year in which he employs Brigitte? What are they?

>

- Matthew fails to adequately confront Brigitte about her failure to generate any income for his business, even while he continues to pay her the remuneration of a saleswoman. Why is he so ineffective at confronting her over this issue?

>

■ Matthew eventually asks Brigitte to leave his business. What view might he have of her after her departure?

The next set of questions invites you to analyze the political issues surrounding Matthew and Brigitte's style differences:

■ To what extent do the unmanaged style differences between Matthew and Brigitte contribute to the breakdown in their working relationship?

■ Given the style differences between them, what could Brigitte have done differently and better to manage her working relationship with her employer?

■ Given the style differences between them, what could Matthew have done differently and better to manage his working relationship with his employee?

MATTHEW AND BRIGITTE: LEARNING FROM THEIR MISTAKES

The final section of this chapter provides a summary of the key issues that Matthew and Brigitte mishandled. Each of the bullet points below relates, in order, to each of the questions above. You might like to read each answer and compare it with the notes that you jotted down. Let's look at the political issues from Brigitte's viewpoint first:

■ Brigitte operates out of a number of hidden agendas during the year. What are they?

Firstly, Brigitte has a significant fear of failure, one that drives her, ultimately, to fail because she won't address it. Her fear of failure affects her early in her employment with Matthew. She is terrified to discover that her sales contacts are not impressed with her new role and don't appear to be interested in her initial overtures to them. She fails to confront her inner fears and buries them almost immediately. This means that she never addresses her strong anxiety, and starts to avoid her two key role goals of selling and learning dressmaking. She therefore avoids her responsibility to her employer to engage in these activities, busies herself with other less threatening tasks, and hopes that Matthew will be satisfied with her performance anyway. When he isn't, and keeps reminding her of her role requirements, she becomes more and more evasive and difficult to deal with. She thinks the issue is that her employer is being unreasonable and is failing to notice just how hard she is working. Actually, the issue is not with Matthew at all. It is internal to her. It is her fear of failure which is so strong that it precludes her from asking for help, from taking the risk of learning anything new, from developing the skills her employer expects her to acquire or from asking her employer for input. Because she won't try, she does fail and he asks her to leave.

Secondly, Brigitte has a significant mistrust agenda. On principle she does not trust Matthew, and believes that he will not remain committed to her as an employee if she tells him how much she is struggling to sell or learn dressmaking. When she takes on the job, Brigitte expects to succeed. But soon into her new employment she gets a rude awakening. She hadn't realized just how difficult it would be for her to learn a new set of skills. She bites off much more than she can chew, but cannot admit this to herself or to her employer. She is used to succeeding and, lacking the maturity or humility to admit she is struggling, she tries to bluff her way through. Even when her manager offers her needed help, she refuses to trust him or his judgment, and rejects the learning opportunities he gives her. She simply doesn't know how to handle the confusing mixture of lowered self-esteem and fear of failure that result from her new role being much more difficult for her than she thought it would be. The issue she faces is not, as she thinks, about Matthew and whether he will or won't support her. It is actually internal to her and is about the fact that she won't put her mistrust agenda sufficiently to one side to take advantage of the fact that he *will* support her if she tries to learn the new skills she needs in her role. As someone who has extended considerable trust to her by employing her on her say-so alone, Matthew expects her to extend some trust back to him. When she doesn't, it is very hard for him. Eventually, after months of trying to get her to sell, after offering her training and trying to get her to talk with him about the challenges of her learning curve, he loses patience with her and does come to mistrust her.

Thirdly, Brigitte is driven by a hidden need for approval. For the first three months of her work for Matthew, when things go well for her, Matthew is pleased with her contribution, and she is buoyant and energized. But, although Brigitte presents herself as confident and competent, her self-esteem is actually not that robust when things start to go wrong for her. When her sales contacts don't jump at the chance to work with her and her new employer, Brigitte doesn't know how to respond and feels dejected. Instead of talking about her dejection with her employer, and enlisting his help so that she can reapproach them, perhaps in tandem with him, she buries her feelings and ignores her responsibility to generate income for his business. Instead, she starts to look for other useful things to do in his shop and office and, being resourceful and bright, finds plenty to keep her occupied. But, this isn't what Matthew is paying her to do, and while this strategy might be more comfortable for Brigitte than the risks of selling or learning something new, it results in Matthew becoming disappointed in her, and she eventually loses his approval. Without anyone actively approving of her work, and seeing it as valuable, Brigitte becomes rebellious and rude to her employer, and feels intimidated by his clients, with whom she is offhand. She thinks that Matthew is the problem, and that he doesn't appreciate her effort and hard work. Actually, the issue is not Matthew. It is her internal agenda that he approve of her all the time, even if she isn't doing what he hired her to do or is paying her to do, which is sell and make dresses. As an employer, he cannot approve of an employee who behaves like this and she consequently does lose his approval.

- Throughout her year's employment with Matthew Brigitte makes a number of political misjudgments. What are her most significant miscalculations?

Brigitte doesn't understand just how important it is to Matthew that she generates sales income for his business. She doesn't listen carefully enough to the reasons why he changes his mind and decides to hire her after initially saying no to her. She fails to understand that her promise to sell his business into new markets is the decisive factor that influences him to provide her with employment. She doesn't appreciate that when her sales contacts don't seem interested in her new role, working in the shop puts her in a parlous position with her boss. Even when he tells her straight that he doesn't want an expensive overhead, she still fails to hear him and doesn't address the issue that he is raising with her, that she is being paid to sell, and needs to do just that. She thinks that running the shop and office for him will free up more time for Matthew to work on client orders, and that he will consequently value her as an employee. She is comfortable that this is enough to justify her salary. She doesn't appreciate sufficiently that, in Matthew's mind, it isn't. Brigitte's subsequent unilateral decision that it is Matthew's job to keep her employed, in return for which she will work hard doing whatever she can for him in the shop and office, is a serious misjudgment on her part. It is a decision which meets her internal agenda of not having to learn anything new, while making a useful contribution, but it does not take into account her boss's wishes or his expectations in employing her.

■ Brigitte did actually want to continue to work with Matthew beyond the first year of her employment. What could she have done to preserve her working relationship with him?

Brigitte needs to be open and honest with her supportive employer in order to preserve his belief in her. She needs to take a risk and trust that, if she talks about some of her worries with him, he will remain supportive of her and committed to her while she climbs a challenging learning curve. Brigitte hopes that if she refuses to discuss her concerns with him, stalls and ignores her responsibility to sell, these issues will go away. They don't. They remain unresolved for Matthew, even if Brigitte does manage not to have to talk about them too often. If she had been prepared to discuss her fears with him she could have opened up a dialog with Matthew and enlisted his support. She could have asked him for input to assist her in re-approaching her contacts. She could have used his sales experience to make a second, and possibly more successful, approach to her contacts. She should also have agreed to attend the dressmaking course and accompany Matthew to the DC sales trip. These actions would have demonstrated to her employer that she wanted to succeed, and would have enabled her to start to confront and defeat her own fears. By failing to try and learn new skills she made it very difficult for Matthew to continue to have faith in her; by failing to confront her own fears about herself she let her anxiety control her behavior, and avoided opportunities to learn her new role competently.

■ Brigitte struggles with an internal conflict throughout the latter part of her employment with Matthew. What is the nature of her internal conflict?

Brigitte's self-image involves seeing herself as capable, competent and able to meet any eventuality. When her attempts to sell her new employer's products to her long-time sales contacts don't even elicit a reply, she immediately doubts herself and fears failing. She cannot afford to see herself as a failure, so she starts to avoid all situations in which she might fail. As she has just started a new job, this means avoiding any situation in which she has to learn something new; she won't attend the dressmaking course and won't accompany Matthew on the DC sales trip. She decides to tackle only those activities that she already knows she is competent at, such as managing the shop and handling the Open House logistics. As well as fearing failure Brigitte struggles to trust other people. When she needs input from Matthew and won't be able to complete a task without it, she still won't ask for help or accept any help he spontaneously offers. Matthew wants to help her succeed, and, despite her refusal to go on the dressmaking course or travel to DC, continues to look for opportunities to help her make the grade. However, her self-image involves seeing herself as autonomous and independent, so she refuses all his offers of help, and, without input, can't meet his high expectations of her and, sadly for her, does fail.

Let's now take a look at the political dynamics from Matthew's viewpoint:

■ When he offers her a job, Matthew takes Brigitte's claims about herself at face value. What are his biggest miscalculations about her?

Firstly, when Matthew hires her, he misjudges Brigitte's confidence as a sign that she possesses both the courage and the will to learn a new profession. Actually, she doesn't have the character to persevere at learning the skills she needs to make a go of in her new role, and gives up very easily. Matthew assumes, wrongly, that given time she'll make the grade, and continues to have patience with her. In reality, Brigitte doesn't have the dedication or the maturity to learn how to sell, design or make his dresses, and Matthew's faith in her is ultimately misplaced.

Secondly, when Matthew hires her, he doesn't want to add to his own workload by having to manage Brigitte or coach her. He expects her to stand alone, and be a proactive, independent and self-motivated employee, an image she projects while persuading him to employ her. He has high expectations of her capacity to set targets for herself and subsequently meet them. He doesn't really consider the possibility that she might not be used to functioning on her own, without an infrastructure around her to support her work, and that her confidence is, in part at least, founded on her being part of an effective retail sales *team* that provides her with much needed support, ideas, contacts and sales material. He doesn't realize that, on her own, she will quickly feel lost and out of her depth and not know how to handle these feelings.

■ Matthew makes a number of errors of judgment as a manager throughout the year in which he employs Brigitte? What are they?

Firstly, Matthew is too close to the situation to see what is really going on with Brigitte. He doesn't recognize her irresponsibility toward him as the political agenda it is, and he misinterprets her dip in confidence as an issue over which he ought to try and support her. When she starts to avoid her responsibility to sell, he thinks it is his job as the employer to help her by offering her suitable development opportunities. It won't matter what forms of development he offers her because the issue is not the timing or content of the development opportunity; it is her inner conflict, a conflict that only she can address. He doesn't realize that, after her long-time sales contacts don't reply to her initial e-mail, Brigitte decides to avoid all opportunities to sell or learn, so that she doesn't have to face her fear of failure. Instead of holding her accountable for her failure to meet her role goals of selling and generating income, he tries to 'help' her with offers of training courses, sales trips and more time to learn about fabrics and dresses from books. All this does is reinforce Brigitte's irresponsibility. As long as the business is doing well, and she can find something useful to do in the shop or office, she is quite happy being paid to do a sales job she isn't doing, and is quite happy letting Matthew fret over the 'right' way to develop her. He does the hard work of trying to solve the problem for her, and she continues to avoid her responsibility to her employer.

Secondly, Matthew is by nature sympathetic and empathic. He notices that Brigitte is struggling, and is losing self-esteem and confidence. But, he is oversensitive to her plight and is consequently too lenient with her. She learns early on in her dealings with Matthew that it is easy for her to deflect him from difficult issues that he wants to raise with her. All she needs to do is offer him practical help, make a useful suggestion or come up with a good idea, and he switches tack and follows her train of thought, instead of remaining committed to his own. She knows he doesn't want to put her on the spot and doesn't like conflict. She learns early on to take advantage of these features of his style, something she does on a regular basis when things start to go wrong for her.

- Matthew fails to adequately confront Brigitte about her failure to generate any income for his business, even while he continues to pay her the remuneration of a saleswoman. Why is he so ineffective at confronting her over this issue?

Matthew has a hard time confronting issues and doesn't like conflict. He extends considerable goodwill to Brigitte throughout their dealings with one another and, foolishly, assumes goodwill still exists in the relationship both ways long after Brigitte starts to avoid her responsibility to sell. Her failure to undertake sales activity is actually a clear sign that she is not thinking about her responsibilities to her employer and therefore isn't offering him any goodwill at all. He prefers working relationships characterized by rapport and harmony, but, because he doesn't want to fall out with his only employee, he uses the third and fourth styles ineffectively. He is permissive instead of understanding (style three) and compliant instead of adaptable (style four). His inability to set Brigitte targets, and hold her accountable for achieving them, creates a situation in which Brigitte can busy herself in the shop and office instead of learning the new skills she needs to learn.

- Matthew eventually asks Brigitte to leave his business. What view might he have of her after her departure?

Matthew's perception of Brigitte might be seriously undermined by her failure to identify, address and resolve her political agendas and internal conflicts. Consequently, he might see her as someone who made false claims about her skills, contacts and determination to succeed in order to get a job. He might see her as someone who lacks the maturity to work autonomously, who is manipulative and who doesn't take responsibility for her actions.

Let's now take a look at the political issues surrounding their style differences:

■ To what extent do the unmanaged style differences between Matthew and Brigitte contribute to the breakdown in their working relationship?

The style issues between Matthew and Brigitte are not the pivotal issues in the breakdown of their relationship, but they do make the management of the relationship much more difficult. The relationship breaks down because Brigitte does not come up to Matthew's expectations of her. She fails in her promise to take his business into new markets and fails to generate any income for him. Matthew's style is goal-orientated toward his own work, but wholly relationship-orientated toward his employee. His people-orientated management of Brigitte means that he continues to support her when he'd be better off holding her accountable for her failure to deliver. It also means that he doesn't set her clear targets or goals to reach. This is a problem for Brigitte. When at her best, Brigitte's style is a mixture of the first and second styles and is highly goal-focused. When under pressure, she uses the second style only, but does so ineffectively because she is afraid of making mistakes. She quickly loses sight of her objective and becomes highly risk-averse, over-analyzes and stalls, sticking her head in the sand instead of taking action or seeking input and advice. On her own, she isn't going to be able to set targets for herself and meet them. Matthew needs to step in at the times when she stalls and set clear targets for her, targets which they jointly evaluate on a regular basis.

■ Given their style differences, what could Brigitte have done differently and better to manage her working relationship with her employer?

Brigitte would have helped her cause significantly had she been open with her employer about the difficulties she was having adjusting to her new role. This would have enabled Matthew to coach her and adopt the role of being a supportive mentor to her. In return Brigitte would have received needed input which might have helped her up a steep learning curve and enabled her to reach her goals and preserve some of her self-esteem and self-confidence.

■ Given their style differences, what could Matthew have done differently and better to manage his working relationship with his employee?

Matthew would have been better off setting delivery targets for Brigitte, and measuring her progress against them. This approach would have given her a set of factual criteria against which to evaluate her progress and would have made discussing her performance issues much easier for both of them, and much more straightforward for her. Without clear criteria against which to judge her performance, she thinks he is being arbitrary in not renewing her contract, and thinks he doesn't understand just how hard she has worked in the shop and in the office. He thinks she doesn't understand commercial reality and doesn't feel any obligation to help him make enough income to cover her salary.

This case study has focused on how an unresolved internal conflict in one person, coupled with unmanaged style differences between her and her manager, can result in the breakdown of a working relationship and loss of employment for one of them.

The following chapter changes tack. It will introduce you to the first of two sets of effective tools that should help you work with your colleagues to get things done, help you make the most of the political influence you could have in any given workplace situation and enable you to use politics positively to achieve the goals of your role when you need to work in tandem with others.

The Political Roles People Play: Getting Things Done with Others

The case study from the last chapter illustrated how one woman struggling with a series of interconnected, unresolved inner conflicts ultimately undermined her own performance, lost the faith of her boss, and subsequently lost her job too. So far we have examined politics in terms of the challenges caused by style issues and hidden agendas. And we have mainly focused on the political dynamics in play between two or three individual colleagues at a time. Let's now widen out our discussion to examine how to get things done effectively when you are working in tandem with several other colleagues at any one time. This chapter, and Chapters 7–9, will focus on the politics of working positively with other people and, when forming political alliances to get things done, on how to work in ways that give you the best chance of bringing your plans to fruition.

GARNERING SUPPORT, FORMING ALLIANCES

Assuming that your plans fall fairly and squarely within your role goals, how do you go about garnering support for your ideas and making them reality? How do you assess what tactics to use to gather support for your plans and handle potential opposition to them successfully? How do you form an effective strategy to help you navigate the political landscape and bring your plans to fruition? This chapter will examine how to step back from your proposals and construct a workable plan to help you:

- Assess the political climate surrounding your proposals.
- Decide whose support you might need.
- Identify who might scupper your plans and how to handle those people should they try to do so.
- Recognize who might be willing to form an alliance with you to help you progress your proposals, however fragile and transitory the partnership.

■ Determine what you need to do to make progress in turning your proposals into concrete action.

This chapter is for you if you want to avoid the possibility of miscalculating the political temperature, misreading the political dynamics or misjudging the political stance that your key colleagues might take and consequently suffer the same fate as the two characters in the last chapter.

DETERMINING THE ROLES PEOPLE PLAY

You work in a role where your ability to get things done is intimately connected to your ability to form and maintain effective working relationships with other people: your colleagues and, in some cases, people from other organizations that you work with, such as your customers. Your colleagues may work in the same department as you, or they may work in a different department to you. They may be your peers or seniors, or they may be more junior to you. Whichever way it works, you cannot get done the things you'd like to get done without the active commitment and support of people within these groups. Making an accurate assessment about who is likely to support you on any given initiative, who is likely to oppose you and who is likely to be ambivalent toward your proposals – at least at first – is key to you making the right approach to the right person at the right time. You will also need to spend time thinking about which influencing tools to use with each person, and Chapter 8 will give you food for thought about how to make effective approaches to key people. But, even with clear ideas about who to approach in which way, you're still not there yet. You need to understand the roles that different people will play *in relation to one another and your proposals* throughout the life cycle of your project so that you can manage the political dynamics effectively. This chapter will show you how.

Example One: Interpersonal Dynamics

Consider the following example set in a small company that sells advertising space on the Internet. The company consists of five full-time employees. The owner of the business is concerned about a growing number of missed sales opportunities, and about the fact that a number of existing customers have recently switched to a rival company. He decides that he wants to change the way in which his firm handles its customers, frames its services to them and handles their post-sales enquiries. Specifically, he wants to move away from the current structure where his employees have defined roles – international sales manager, national sales manager, IT manager and office manager – and move toward a structure where each employee manages a number of accounts from first sales contact onwards. He believes that the business relationships that his staff will build with their customers using this structure will create more long-term business. He spends time talking to each member of his team one by one, taking them through his plans and telling them what the changes will mean for them:

- The international sales manager is in favor of the idea. She talks about it positively straightaway and, after meeting with the business owner, speaks favorably about his proposals to her colleagues in the office. The change in business structure means that she needs to learn new IT and account management skills, and she sees this as an opportunity to be taken advantage of. She agrees that the company needs to act sooner rather than later to make sure that it retains its valued customers, and is worried that, if it doesn't succeed in doing this, it might go under.
- The national sales manager isn't in favor of the plan at all. He likes his current job, doesn't want it to change and doesn't want to learn anything new. The national sales manager doesn't see the need to make radical changes to the structure of the firm. He's been an employee for ten years and seen hard times before. He thinks the firm should stick to what it knows best, keep doing it and that, in the end, they'll come through fine. While his employer values him for his sales skills and honesty, he is frustrated by his apparent reluctance to learn anything new and by his own inability to influence his employee to see the benefits of his plans.
- The IT manager is cautious about the new plans. She likes the idea of a more people-facing role and the variety that this will bring to her working life. But she is nervous about having to sell. She hasn't any experience of doing so and is not that confident that she'll be any good at it. She tells her employer that she'll have a go if he wants, but that she'll need to be convinced that she can sell before she'll make a live call. She worries that if she's no good at selling, despite her having worked for the firm for six years, she'll lose her job.
- The office manager is tepid about the proposals. He says that he agrees something needs to be done, but points out that all the relationships will change and people will become competitors of one another for client business, something which isn't an issue at the

moment. He suggests to his employer that the character of the office might change and not for the better. Over the next two days he comments to his three colleagues, quietly and confidentially, that he thinks there is more to the proposals than their employer is letting on, and that they need to watch their backs. The office manager has long wanted to run his own business, but has never had the courage to do so.

Example One: A Political Framework

In this example the owner of the firm has taken on the role of persuading his employees to learn new skills and adopt different roles in order to, as he sees it, ensure the survival of his business. Assuming that he wants to keep all his staff – and he does – he will need to tailor his approach to influencing each of them based on his reading of their initial reaction to those proposals. His first step is to decide which political role each person is adopting on the issue. To help him do this effectively he might want to use the following tool which is a framework for determining the political roles people take at work. I have adapted it from an unattributed model I was introduced to years ago by a client. The framework uses some of the concepts presented in their model by Tuckner Consulting Inc. You will see that there are five possible positions on the framework:

- Core team members.
- Supporters.
- Fence-sitters.
- Opponents.
- Adversaries.

The business owner needs to decide which stance each of his staff is adopting. To do this he needs to form a view on two key factors. These are the degree to which he believes that

- each of his employees is working toward the same role goals as he is
- his relationship with each employee is characterized by mutual regard, and that he respects each person and likes their values and ways of working.

Take a look at the Figure 6.1 below:

The framework operates on an issue by issue basis which means that the same person could play two different roles on two different issues, i.e. one person could be a supporter on one issue and an

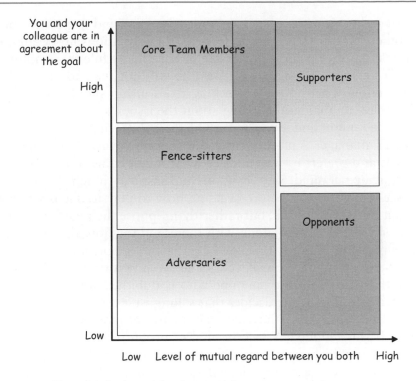

Figure 6.1   The political roles people adopt at work

opponent on another issue, or a fence-sitter on one issue and an adversary on another. Put yourself in the shoes of the business owner and decide which of the four employees you'd place in which category. You might like to write their role description on the appropriate place on the framework.

Example One: Analyzing the Political Dynamics

Compare what you have written with the following analysis:

- The international sales manager is a supporter of the proposals. She wants to see the company act to retain its customers and therefore has the same goal in mind as her employer. She is open minded and enthusiastic about learning new skills, and promotes her boss's proposals when speaking with her colleagues in the office.
- The national sales manager is an opponent of the proposals. He and his employer have different aims on this issue. The business owner wants to change the structure of the company to retain its customers; the national sales manager doesn't see the need and would prefer

to sit tight. However, they have mutual regard and respect for one another. This is an important feature of the relationship because it means that the business owner can be sure that while this employee won't actively champion his plans, he will not try and undermine them either. Their effective working relationship should also mean that they can maintain a dialog about the issues between them, and that they might find a way to resolve their differences.

- The IT manager is a fence-sitter. She is ambivalent about the proposals and prefers to wait and see what might come of them before making up her mind. She is cautious and suspends judgment, waiting to see what happens before deciding how to play it. She is worried about her ability to sell, but rather than oppose the plans straightaway she decides to go along with them and see how they pan out. This reaction buys her time, and creates the opportunity for her to test the water with her colleagues and see how they react. She may find that she is not the only one who is dubious, and that she has readymade allies if she decides that selling isn't for her.

- The office manager is an adversary of the proposals, but a clever one. To his employer's face he makes insightful comments about the way in which the character of the company might change if the proposals become reality. Behind his employer's back he suggests to his colleagues that there might be more going on than the business owner has let on, although he has no evidence for this and, if pressed, will have nothing further to add. He wants to spread discontent, and takes advantage of the uncertainty created by the proposals to drop uncomfortable ideas into the minds of his colleagues, ideas designed to make them doubt their employer for whom he feels jealousy and envy.

You'll note that in the example above there is no one who the business owner would ascribe to the core team member category. Should the scenario have been set in a larger company, and the action have centered on cross-departmental issues, then some of the characters might have sat comfortably in the core team member category too, as you'll see from the descriptions below.

RECOGNIZING THE POLITICAL ROLES PEOPLE PLAY

Now that we've digested the way in which the framework operates let's take a more in-depth look at the distinctions between the five possible categories, and the way in which the framework relates to your working world. Remember that the framework operates issue by issue, so one particular colleague might play different roles on different issues. Also, you don't have to ascribe people to every category on every issue you consider. In some situations you may not have any supporters, or you may only have fence-sitters and so on.

Let's start by taking an in-depth look at the five possible political stances identified by the framework.

Core Team Members: Similar Role Goals, but Not Always Mutual Regard

- Your core team members are people who are part of your main team or group, and are therefore likely to be people with whom you work day-to-day. Your working relationships are structured around achieving the same goals so you are likely to be working together on similar or related tasks and objectives. You are likely to want to work together to keep your relationships on an even keel. You'll notice that the category extends from one end of the horizontal axis almost to the other. You could be candid about some matters with people who you place at the right-hand edge of the category, but not with people who you place on the left-hand edge. You will need to be more judicious about what you communicate to some of the people in this category than others, depending upon the level of mutual regard you believe exists in the relationship; and on your best understanding of the degree to which they are actively and solely engaged in meeting the same role goals as you. When speaking with core team members, you could openly acknowledge that you are on the same side and have much in common, but that sometimes you will need to be selective about what you say to them, based on the sensitivity of the issues involved.

Supporters: Similar Role Goals and Mutual Regard

- People who you place in your supporters category are likely to be colleagues with whom you have a history of mutual regard. You have worked well together in the past and, crucially, believe that you are pursuing similar role goals on this particular issue. Your supporters are not usually part of your core team but are people elsewhere in the organization with whom you have a track record of effective collaboration. What makes them supporters on this particular issue is that they have similar, or the same, role goals as you and honor their relationship with you. On other issues they may or may not be your supporters, but on this issue you consider them to be working with you toward the same aims and in ways you like. This means that, in a meeting with them about the issues, you can begin by speaking about the issues on which you are in agreement with one another. You can highlight the quality of the relationship that you have built up with one another, and remind them about past successful partnerships between you. You can go on to be clear about any concerns you have, and engage in a problem-solving conversation to resolve these issues, knowing that your mutual regard will ensure that these are safe discussions to have.

Opponents: Mutual Regard, but Dissimilar Role Goals

■ People who you regard as opponents are likely to be those with whom you have a history of successful collaboration, but who have different goals to you on this particular issue. The goals they are pursuing are not in line with your role goals. It's a bit like a tennis match, you may like and respect your opponent but you still want to beat them. Opponents are generally people for whom you have positive regard. You have time for their views and think they handle things with integrity. However, you have opposing viewpoints to them or seek a different outcome to them on this particular issue. But, because the quality of the relationship you have with them is good, you do have a way forward. You can start any meeting with them by affirming that the relationship is based on mutual regard and that in the past you have worked well together. You can say that you anticipate doing so again in the future. You could then go on to state your position on the current issue in terms of your desired goal, the process you want to follow to get there and an explanation of why you want to proceed in this way. You could also state in a nonevaluative way what you think their position is before, crucially, engaging them in a problem-solving process about points of disagreement. Hopefully, you will find a way of resolving at least some of the issues between you.

Fence-sitters: Little Mutual Regard, Dissimilar Role Goals

■ People who you regard as fence-sitters are likely to be those who either don't know what they want in regard to this issue, or those who do know what they want but find it advantageous not to say so. Fence-sitters are very hard to judge. They may form the biggest group for some of you, especially for those of you who work for larger organizations. Fence-sitters tend to remain noncommittal and vague about what they want. They tend not to be frank or open, and often wait and see what happens before declaring their support for whichever side they think it will be advantageous to join. Fence-sitters tend to make few definitive statements, give little away, express few clear opinions and, even when they do, often change their minds afterwards. They tend not to give direct answers to direct questions. When dealing with a fence-sitter you need to exercise caution. You may be tempted to try and convert fence-sitters into supporters. Don't. It doesn't work. Fence-sitters don't want to make commitments and prefer to keep their business relationships loose and ill-defined. This gives them room for maneuver. When working with a fence-sitter you might begin by stating your position clearly in terms of what you want to do and why you want to do it. You might then want to talk about your goal and the process you want to follow to achieve it. You could ask them where they stand and what they want to achieve. You may not get a straight answer, but you ought to get a few clues about who they are listening to, whose views influence them or what specific factors sway them. If you are lucky, you may get a concrete answer to a question and, if you do, and you don't like what you hear, you may want to try and influence them toward seeing your point of view. However, don't waste too much time or energy trying to convert them – let them go and move on.

Adversaries: Dissimilar Role Goals, No Mutual Regard

■ You may or may not have people in your adversaries category. Adversaries are people with whom you share very little. You do things differently to them, don't like the way they operate and, on this issue, have completely different goals to them. Worse, you believe that, as far as this issue goes, they are actively working against you. When dealing with adversaries don't give away information. It is the political currency they need and want, and the more you give away the less you have left. You could state your goal and the process you want to follow. You could state your best understanding of what they want in as nonevaluative way as you can manage. You could identify your own contribution to any tensions which exist. But, basically, that's it. Keep meetings with your adversaries short. You aren't going to make business friends with your adversaries. Adversarial business relationships are just that: relationships with people who are your business foes and who want you to lose. Don't spend much time with them. Spend it with your supporters instead.

PLANNING YOUR STRATEGY: A CASE STUDY FROM YOUR WORKING LIFE

You might now like to select a case study from your own working life so that you can formulate a strategy for how you might handle the issues in it using the framework above. The case study you select needs to be about an issue at work that is important to you, and one which involves several key colleagues. You might want to select a case study where you are actively seeking support for a particular project, initiative or idea that you have originated. Consider each of the key players involved in the situation in turn and decide which category you will place them in based on the role descriptions above. You might like to write the names of each of the key players in the space below the category you have placed them in.

- Supporters:

- Core team members:

- Fence-sitters:

- Opponents:

- Adversaries:

You might now like to read through the following pointers about how to handle people you've placed in each of the categories. You could jot down any specific ideas, tactics or strategies that come to mind in the space below each pointer. The aim of this exercise is to help you decide the most influential way of approaching each person so that you have the best chance of bringing your plans to fruition.

- Invest time with your supporters: spend time talking with your supporters. They are your business allies; they share similar views to you; and you believe that they are pursuing the same role goals as you. You could meet with them to review progress on the key issues, identify future challenges and risks, plan a way forward and decide how to capitalize on the opportunities you jointly perceive to exist.

```



```

- Open discussions with your opponents: you need to explore the possibility of finding common ground with this group of people. As you consider your opponents to be basically decent people, albeit people with a different goal in mind to you, you can invest time profitably in discussing the issues between you. Remembering that mutual regard exists between you, your opponents are unlikely to use any information they gain in these meetings against you, and are unlikely to take advantage of their relationship with you. You may also find ways of influencing them during these meetings, or of coming to a better understanding of why they are committed to a different outcome to you.

```



```

- Touch base with your core team members: you could cautiously find out where each of the people in your core team stands on the key issues, using your shared interests as a starting point for the discussion. Your aim in arranging these meetings could be to make decisions about which of your core team members, if you have any, will be most likely to work profitably with you to bring about the outcomes you want.

```



```

- Don't invest time speaking with the fence-sitters: fence-sitters won't talk openly with you, they won't make commitments to you that they intend to keep, they won't be frank with you about their views and they won't be convinced by you either. You will not be able to do a deal with them, negotiate with them, exchange real views with them or come to an agreement with them. Don't waste your time or effort on them. It won't be rewarded. Invest your energies elsewhere instead.

- Don't dialog with your adversaries: the more you tell them, the stronger they become. Instead state your position as clearly and simply as you can, but don't make any concessions to them, demand anything from them or offer them anything either.

YOUR POLITICAL BEHAVIOR

You may now like to examine your own political behavior using the framework. You could select a recent workplace issue which involves you, but one which you have not initiated. It might be a situation in which someone senior to you is proposing changes which affect you, and you need to respond to their proposals. Consider the following questions:

- What is your initial reaction to the issue?

- Looking at it from your senior colleague's point of view, which political role are you adopting on this issue?

> ⬛ What impact does this stance have on your working relationship with the senior manager and any other key people involved in the issue?

> ⬛ If you are in this situation again what, if anything, would you do differently?

SUMMARY AND NEXT CHAPTER

This chapter has focused on the political roles that you and your colleagues adopt at work. It has highlighted a variety of roles and stances that different people – and you – can play at work. In particular, it has examined five different political roles and demonstrated how to identify which colleague is playing which role in any given situation. The chapter has included an opportunity for you to apply this structured way of examining workplace political roles to a real-life situation from your own working life, and develop a workable strategy to enable you to maximize your influence in a situation you are initiating. It has also included an opportunity for you to apply the framework to a second situation at work, and look at your own political behavior through the eyes of a senior manager.

The following case study builds on these themes. It focuses on what happens when two ambitious young managers, who work for an older manager they do not respect, decide to launch a new training initiative. They do so without involving their manager fully enough in their plans, or understanding the political consequences of their actions for him. It illustrates the pitfalls for the young managers of failing to understand the political roles that they adopt as far as their manager is concerned and of failing to take into account the prevailing political climate when initiating plans and proposals that affect their boss and the wider organization.

In-House Values Initiative

BACKGROUND AND CHARACTERS

This case study is set in the hotel industry in Auckland, New Zealand. The three principal characters work in Head Office. The hotel group has been through a challenging time during the past six months due to a rival company opening up higher quality establishments at a lower tariff in similar locations. While no one has been made redundant, and the Board are keen to avoid losing even one member of their staff, the in-house Innovations Team have been working overtime to find creative ways of upgrading the value of their offer to their customers, so that they don't need to get into a price war with their new rival. Their remit – one that has been given to them by the Board – is to roll out a high-profile Values Initiative to all ten hotels in the group built around three corporate values: Delivering for Customers, Exceeding Customer Expectations and Working Together. The Innovations Team have been working on the proposed roll out of the Values Initiative for several months now and nearly ready to commence delivering it.

The Innovations Team is run by Walter and is a small but tight unit of ten people. Walter reports straight to the Board and makes sure that when he has received a brief from the senior team, no one in any of the hotels hears about it until he is ready to roll it out. Walter is the longest-serving member of the group's workforce. While not renowned for his own creativity or energy, he is an efficient, if controlling, manager and has managed the effective roll out of three group initiatives in the past 20 months. Each of these projects involved a roll out in all ten hotels by his team members strictly according to his plan and timescales. The two most active members of his team are Soraya and Brent, both of whom are young, both of whom are ambitious and both of whom are frustrated at what they see as their manager's old school and overprotective approach to his role. They worry that his style prevents them from meeting senior managers, from gaining influence and from making as rapid progress as they might otherwise do. They have formed the view that he is treading water until he retires in three years time.

Walter is undeniably old school. He is unwilling or unable to let go and, for an industry that is constantly inventive, he appears, to his staff at any rate, out-of-date and unoriginal. However, he does deliver and has a strong relationship with the Board, a relationship he jealously guards from his staff who he doesn't invite to attend Board Meetings with him. Walter privately admits to himself that he is biding his time until he retires. He dislikes Soraya and Brent, thinks they are too pushy, too full of ideas and too quick to rush into things without thinking through what he sees as the delicate political ramifications of the actions they take. In particular, he thinks they are disrespectful to him and his position in the group. Secretly, he feels threatened by them and senses that they'd prefer to work for someone who'd give them more leeway and greater responsibility.

Soraya reports to Walter. She is enthusiastic, energetic, not very mature, not at all politically astute and more forthright than is good for her. She can misjudge situations and she shows her feelings too readily. She despises Walter, thinks he is a stick-in-the-mud, and while that would be ok – just about – she is constantly riled by his deliberate strategy of not allowing his team members to meet or work with people more influential than him. While Walter doesn't say no directly, he tends to sit on requests he wants to block, or asks for unnecessary preparation and research to be done in advance of giving his decision. Soraya hates this way of doing things, and thinks it a waste of her time and effort and a drain on her enthusiasm. Soraya is completely behind the new values and excited at the prospect of being involved in the roll out. She sees the roll out as a big opportunity for her to meet and work with hotel managers and staff, and is worried that Walter might prevent her from playing as full a part in the delivery of the project as her work on its design might warrant. She complains to Brent about Walter's style on a regular basis as a way of venting her frustration.

Brent is a peer of Soraya's and also reports to Walter. He is able interpersonally, enjoys working as part of a team, is outgoing and is better at reading people than Soraya. He is savvy enough to be respectful to Walter when he speaks with him, and is careful enough to keep the extent of his frustrations to himself when at work. He understands – even sympathizes with – Soraya's complaints, but thinks she is unwise to voice them as often or as vociferously as she does. He also believes in the new values and is excited at the prospect of traveling to the hotel locations to roll out the program and meet new colleagues.

Walter, for all his frustrations at managing the two of them, thinks that Soraya and Brent make a good team. He believes that Soraya's goal focused and somewhat driven style works well alongside Brent's more thoughtful and people-orientated style. Soraya and Brent also enjoy working together and openly acknowledge between them that Brent is the more interpersonally astute of the two of them.

THE ROLL OUT OF THE VALUES INITIATIVE

Walter draws up a clear and thorough plan for designing, delivering and evaluating the roll out of the Values Initiative to the ten hotels in the group. When he presents his plan to his team, Soraya and Brent in particular are dismayed at their lack of involvement in the overall management of the roll out, which is being completely handled by Walter. Their role is limited to jointly delivering Values Workshops to staff at three hotels. While fully behind the initiative, they are not on board with the plan to deliver it and go for a drink after work to talk about how to handle their chagrin with their boss.

THE WEEK BEFORE THE ROLL OUT COMMENCES

Without checking this out with Walter, Soraya and Brent decide to call each of the hotel managers and deputies to inform them about the upcoming Values Initiative. Soraya takes five of the hotels and Brent the other five. Their aim in making these calls is to position the upcoming roll out with their senior colleagues, selling the concept and benefits of the program to each hotel manager and deputy. They also want to describe the process and content of the Values Workshops for hotel-based staff and, crucially, make sure that the managers and deputies realize that they, Soraya and Brent, are key to the inception, design and delivery of the initiative. They have worked very hard on the initiative and do know a lot about it. While talking to the hotel managers and deputies Soraya and Brent sound knowledgeable, competent and informed. They answer questions, take notes and promise to get back to their colleagues with additional information. However, in making these calls they are going above the head of their manager and putting themselves on a direct collision course with him. While they never explicitly say to one another that they will make the calls without consulting Walter first, this is in fact what they do. Neither of them thinks to inform him of what they have done afterwards either, and when, over the next 24 hours, Walter starts to get calls from hotel managers and deputies with detailed questions about what will happen and when, he hits the roof.

WALTER'S RESPONSE

Walter is furious. He had intended to send out a briefing pack to each hotel manager from him. The briefing pack would inform them in detail about the timescale of events and the personnel involved at each stage of the roll out process. On realizing that these plans have been preempted, without his knowledge, by his two pushy team members he calls loudly across the office to Brent and Soraya commanding them to come to his office immediately. As they walk toward his now closed door the two colleagues agree to stick together in the meeting that follows.

Walter tells them to sit down and starts by confronting them with the question, 'What do you think you've been doing?' Soraya defends their actions robustly. She says that they should be commended for their proactive and delivery-focused approach. She says that she and Brent have saved Walter a good deal of work, and have done a great job of selling the Values Initiative to the hotels. Walter responds by calling them both 'untrustworthy and politically inept' and describing their actions as 'totally unacceptable'. Soraya tells Walter that he is being unfair and that he should be pleased to have two such hard-working people in his department. She looks at Brent, waiting for him to speak, expecting his verbal support for her stance. But instead he tells Walter that he recognizes he has overstepped the mark, and apologizes. Soraya can't believe what she is hearing, and instead of backing down, she looks mutinously at Brent before telling Walter that he is 'holding her back'. Walter accuses her of being both 'unprofessional and disrespectful' toward him and tells her she is a fool. He orders her out of his office.

A few minutes later Brent leaves Walter's office and walks over to Soraya's desk. He recommends that she apologizes to Walter, and tells her it'd be in her best interests to go and smooth it all over. Soraya tells Brent that he is weak and traitorous, before returning to her work. She doesn't apologize to Walter and, over the next few weeks, finds that the work assigned to her in the department, while never mundane, isn't as stretching or interesting as she was used to. She only visits one hotel during the roll out. Her relationship with Walter remains distant, and her relationship with Brent doesn't recover either. When they work together on joint assignments they are wary of one another and speak only when they absolutely have to. Brent and Walter certainly don't become buddies, but they do work together going forward.

ANALYZING THE POLITICAL DYNAMICS: YOUR ROLE

Consider the following questions. They are designed to help you look behind the facts of the case study and examine the political dynamics at play between Walter, Soraya and Brent. You can jot down your answers to each question in the space below it:

■ What political roles do Soraya and Brent adopt in relation to one another at the start of the case study?

■ What political roles do Soraya and Brent adopt in relation to their manager Walter at the start of the case study?

■ As the action unfolds, and they agree to work together on the telephone calls to the hotels, what political roles do Brent and Soraya adopt toward their manager Walter?

■ Why is Walter so angry with Soraya and Brent for making the pre-calls to the hotel managers and deputies?

■ In what ways do the political roles that Soraya and Brent play in relation to one another alter during the course of their acrimonious meeting with Walter in his office?

[ ]

- What mistakes does Soraya make in that meeting?

[ ]

- What mistakes does Soraya make after the meeting?

[ ]

- What are the key lessons that Soraya and Brent would do well to take away from this episode?

[ ]

LEARNING FROM SORAYA AND BRENT'S MISTAKES

The final section of this chapter provides a summary of the key issues that Soraya and Brent mishandle. Each of the bullet points below relates, in order, to one of the questions above. You might like to read each answer and compare it with the notes that you jotted down:

- What political roles do Soraya and Brent adopt in relation to one another at the start of the case study?

   Soraya and Brent start out as core team members albeit ones who are probably over to the right hand side of the category, and who therefore adopt the role of being supporters of one another. They are similarly ambitious and hardworking, and understand each other's frustrations with Walter's managerial style. They have similar goals to one another for the Values Initiative. They both want to play a full part in the delivery of the program having worked hard on its inception and design.

- What political roles do Soraya and Brent adopt in relation to their manager Walter at the start of the case study?

Initially, they both regard their manager's style with concern. Soraya regards him as a fence-sitter and, foolishly given his seniority, despises him. Brent regards him as a core team member, but places him on the left hand side of the category. They both think they have dissimilar goals to their manager as far as the Values Initiative is concerned. They want to get on, take responsibility and enhance their profiles; they think he wants to squash them and take all the available credit for himself.

- As the action unfolds, and they agree to work together on the telephone calls to the hotels, what political roles do Brent and Soraya adopt toward their manager Walter?

From the moment Walter rolls out his implementation plan, whether they realize it or not – and looking at it from Walter's point of view – both Soraya and Brent become supporters of one another and adversaries of their manager. Their joint aim is to gain higher profile and more responsibility than Walter's blueprint affords them, and in order to achieve this aim they decide to go above his head to the hotel managers and deputies directly. They think their manager is deliberately sidelining them from the action and deliberately reducing their opportunities to impress influential people in the hotel group. While they want the Values Initiative to succeed, they also want to play a major role in its success and gain the credit they believe their behind-the-scenes efforts deserve.

- Why is Walter so angry with Soraya and Brent for making the pre-calls to the hotel managers and deputies?

Walter is a very controlling manager, and feels that he has lost control over a critical aspect of a high-profile project, at an early stage in its delivery, and publicly at that. Brent and Soraya's actions have set the wheels in motion before he is ready to do so, even if only by a week or so. He feels that he has potentially lost credibility with some of the hotel managers and deputies because, although he bluffed well enough, it was obvious to those he spoke with that he didn't know the pre-calls had been made by members of his own department. He is worried that the managers and deputies he spoke with won't waste much time telling other managers and deputies about this interesting development in the Innovations Team. Whether they will or not is not the issue. He *fears* they will and this makes him angry. His anger is partly because he realizes that he should have thought of making the calls himself and didn't, and is partly because, by the sound of it, the way Soraya and Brent have positioned the roll out with the few managers he has spoken with was excellent. He is embarrassed that he didn't know anything about their calls and, secretly, while he realizes he is overreacting, he also fears that unless he comes down hard on both of them, they will in future try something like this – or worse – undermining him further still.

- In what ways do the political roles that Soraya and Brent play in relation to one another alter during the course of their acrimonious meeting with Walter in his office?

Soraya goes into Walter's office thinking that she and Brent are supporters of one another. Being somewhat politically naïve, she thinks they will stand together in the upcoming meeting come what may. Brent, however, knows that their alliance is purely strategic, and while he doesn't intentionally deceive Soraya about his willingness to stand alongside her, he is cute enough to change his mind when the meeting appears to demand it. When Walter's anger is unrelenting, he decides it's every person for himself and backs down. He adopts the role of a respectful core team member toward his boss, which has the unfortunate consequence of resulting in Soraya seeing him as an adversary, not a supporter. Soraya doesn't back down, however, and remains angry with Walter, and doubly so because Brent has let her down. Instead of following his suit and apologizing, she becomes even more strident and presents herself as an implacable adversary of her boss, someone with a different aim from him, and someone who doesn't honor her relationship with him. This is a big mistake because she simply lacks the seniority to go head to head with her own manager, no matter how justified she believes she is in her own mind.

- What mistakes does Soraya make in that meeting?

Soraya makes several mistakes during the meeting. Her first error is that she is unrepentant in the face of Walter's anger, and continues to justify hers and Brent's pre-calls to the hotels without recognizing the political implications for Walter of their joint actions. She could have started off the meeting in a different place, making the same points but doing so in a more respectful and humble way. She could have presented the facts of her case rather than the emotion, and have done so in way that recognized that she had embarrassed her boss. She could have said something like, 'I recognize you must be surprised that we've called the hotels without your knowledge. Our enthusiasm and excitement about the project got the better of us, and we just went ahead without thinking. It wasn't our intention to go over your head, or embarrass you, although I can see that it must look like that. In reality, what we wanted to do was to generate momentum and get things going. We have actually done a good job of selling the initiative to the hotels and they are all geared up and excited about the program. How would you like to handle things from here on in?' This approach would strike a balance between recognizing their wish to take on more responsibility, and recognizing the impact of their precipitate action on their manager, without actually either attacking him or saying they'd done anything wrong. It also hands back control to Walter, putting him in the driving seat. Soraya's second error is that she doesn't take a hint. Rather than learn from Brent's volte-face and back down when she has the opportunity to do so, she takes his apology to Walter as a personal betrayal and becomes even angrier with her boss. She could have diffused the impasse between herself and Walter had she followed Brent's lead and apologized.

- What mistakes does Soraya make after the meeting?

Soraya doesn't think about the situation from anyone's point of view but her own. She demonstrates an unhelpful degree of stubbornness and fails to make peace with her boss or with Brent. Both of her working relationships suffer as a consequence. It is possible that, when he was alone with Walter for the few minutes after Soraya left the meeting, Brent tried to smooth things over on her behalf. His efforts will be in vain unless Soraya finds it in her heart to apologize to her manager, even though he is someone she thinks so little of. It is also possible that, when he apologizes to Walter, Brent fully expects Soraya to follow his lead and do the same. It is openly acknowledged between the two of them that Brent is better at handling people than Soraya. Brent might have been surprised that, following his apology, she doesn't also apologize but continues to attack their boss, starts to see him as an enemy and injures her relationships with both of them. Brent might have thought that in apologizing first – and expecting her to follow suit – he was acting in the best interests of both of them, and he may be disappointed and surprised that his relationship with Soraya doesn't recover from this point on. Soraya could have avoided all these consequences had she backed down gracefully in the meeting with Walter.

■ What are the key lessons that Soraya and Brent would do well to take away from this episode?

Firstly, they need to understand that they cannot take unilateral action in the roles they are in. They are both part of a department which is part of a group of hotels, and what they do affects people and issues beyond themselves. They both need to think about the political impact of their actions on their boss, on his relationships with the hotel managers and deputies and on the quality of their working relationships with him going forward. Just because they don't respect their manager's style or decisions does not give them carte blanche to take action independent of his say-so. They both need to strike a balance between their justifiable wish to be more involved in the roll out and their responsibilities to their manager. After all, he is the one with the authority in the department and the one with the ear of the Board. They need to act in ways that don't incur his wrath even if they don't like or respect his methods. Secondly, they need to realize that Walter's style is quite purposeful and serves his goals effectively. Soraya, in particular, tends to dismiss him, seeing him as ineffective and contemptible. What she doesn't appreciate is that his high need to control is exactly that. He needs and wants to be in control and if anyone disrespects this clear preference, not only will he have something to say about it, he will also act against them to prevent them trying to do so again in future. Thirdly, Soraya needs to realize that until she apologizes to her manager he is unlikely to trust her again, and is therefore likely to keep her on less interesting projects rather than give her full reign in the department as before. Without some acknowledgment on her part that she has acted hastily and unwisely, Walter might not be minded to place her in a position where she could embarrass him again, and might be tempted to keep her office-bound, potentially underutilized and possibly bored and unchallenged. Fourthly, Soraya needs to realize that she isn't the best at sizing up people and situations. She needs to temper her natural forthright and full-on style with a willingness to listen to other people's points of views, and a willingness to hear what they are saying without getting defensive or aggressive. She needs to take the lead from more interpersonally astute colleagues, like Brent, and learn that there are more effective ways of achieving her goals than her no-nonsense and outspoken style.

This case study has focused on the political roles people play at work. It has demonstrated how these can change during the course of one evolving issue, highlighting the impact that adopting, as far as their manager sees it, an adversarial role toward him can have on his working relationships with two members of his team. The case study has specifically examined how a young manager's failure to read the political landscape effectively costs her dearly in her relationship with her manager, and loses her the support of one of her key colleagues. The case study explored the difference between making a political mistake, recognizing its impact on the manager involved and apologizing; and making a political mistake, justifying those actions to the manager involved and thereby compounding the problem by failing to take responsibility for the initial error of judgment. The case study has shown the potential cost of not recognizing the political role you adopt – as far as more influential colleagues are concerned – when formulating plans and implementing them.

The following chapter will build on these themes and examine how to make the most of the sources of influence available to you in the workplace when you set out to work constructively with your colleagues. It will identify a variety of sources of organizational and personal power at work, and illustrate how to call upon these effectively to get things done when working with others.

Power and Politics: Bringing Your Plans to Fruition

The case study from the last chapter illustrated how political misjudgments by two colleagues resulted in them taking ill-advised steps and undermining their relationships with their manager. What they wanted to do – play a role in the launch of a new initiative – was fair enough, but the way in which they went about it let them down. They failed to show sufficient respect for their manager and to think through the political ramifications of their actions both for him and for themselves. If they had taken a different tack – one that involved approaching their manager with their ideas and working with him to get things done in a way he sanctioned – the outcome could have been very different and much better for them. The case study illustrated that, before initiating any significant proposals, you need to consider the impact of your plans on those affected by them, especially those senior to you who have a vested interest in the outcome of your work, and whose opinion of you can be adversely affected if you handle things poorly.

Let's now continue our examination of how to work effectively with other people in your workplace and extend it to include how to use the power available to you in your role to get things done, especially when you:

- Need to work in tandem with other people.
- Want to gain support for plans and proposals that you want to initiate.

This chapter will examine the reality of workplace power; what it is, where it comes from, how to preserve it from colleagues who'd like to take it from you and how to use it to build influence. The chapter will highlight how you can make the most of the organizational and personal power available to you in your role. It will show you how to get the best from the opportunities you have to influence and work effectively with other people, so that you can capitalize on your political currency and make it work for you, not against you. I am quite consciously using the term 'power' in this chapter to distinguish it from tempting euphemisms such as 'responsibility', or 'leadership' or 'managerial influence'.

WORKING WITH OTHERS

You work in a role where you cannot achieve anything on your own. Your ability to get things done, have influence and achieve your goals are all intimately connected to your capacity to work in tandem with other people. Depending on the situation, you might need to work well with one other person or with a variety of people, your peers, your seniors, your team members or other colleagues. Each of these people performs a role which is different from yet interconnected to yours. You cannot take a unilateral decision, because it simply doesn't work that way. You may have bright ideas, but turning your ideas into reality means that you have to influence other people to see it your way, to back you and to work with you. You must work – and be seen to work – with each and every one of your peers, seniors and other colleagues if you are to get anywhere, no matter how valid and valuable your ideas may potentially be to your employer.

However, working with other people carries risks with it and some difficulties too. Your colleagues might work in different ways to you. Some of them might want to take credit for your work. Others might promise to get things done by certain deadlines which they don't subsequently meet. They might tell you that they'll carry out certain tasks to a specific standard but fail to meet that standard. Others again might – in extreme cases – want to injure your reputation or damage your credibility. On the other hand, those very people could also turn out to be stimulating, collaborative, fun and supportive coworkers. However, the reality of being part of the average workplace is that you will, from time to time, have to find ways to work effectively alongside people with whom you may have:

- Nothing at all in common.
- Nothing to talk about apart from work.
- Completely different approaches to workplace issues and relationships.
- Completely different sets of values and priorities.

So in order to get things done with these groups of people you will need to:

- Be mindful of the political landscape around you, protecting your power by judiciously managing your boundaries.
- Understand what influences each of them, what they value at work and what they want to achieve.
- Find individual ways to convince them that it would be in their best interests to listen to what you have to say and to work constructively with you.

This chapter will help you examine your options for maximizing your influence in situations where, if you don't think strategically and tactically before acting, you may well end up unable to achieve what you want, even though your goal is squarely in line with what you are paid to do and could benefit your organization. Specifically, the chapter will help you to distinguish between, and then subsequently explore, three different forms of power at work, personal power, organizational status and organizational influence. It will help you to:

- Understand how to preserve your personal power in challenging workplace relationships.
- Recognize that significant organizational status carries with it significant responsibilities toward your staff.
- Understand who – including you – has access to which source or sources of organizational influence in any given situation.
- Decide how to approach your colleagues so that you can maximize the influence you could have with them on a key workplace issue.

DEFINING PERSONAL POWER AT WORK

Let's start by examining the nature of personal power at work. You might like to jot down any words, images and phrases that the term 'personal power at work' conjures up for you. You can use the space below to write down your thoughts:

Two of the key issues for us in exploring handling politics at work are:

- Why is it that some of you struggle to retain your personal power in some of your working relationships, but experience no such difficulties in other relationships?
- And why is it that others of you again have no difficulty at all in retaining your personal power in all of your relationships?

Look back at what you've written. What pictures do the words and phrases you've used paint? Perhaps you see 'personal power' as something static, unchanging and universal. You might think that you, and everyone else, have a fixed amount of personal power, and that it's the degree that changes from person to person. You might think that, like hair colour or physique, different people are born with differing degrees of personal power, and that this explains why some of you are more apparently able in this area than others of you. Then again, you might see personal power as being something fluid, something that you can give away or acquire, something that your experience of can vary depending on who you are dealing with at the time. In this case you might view personal power as something that you experience only in relation to another person, and that varies with every relationship you are in.

In my opinion, personal power is a potential capacity that everyone is born with, but, just like confidence, the trick is in learning to use behavior which preserves, retains, protects and makes the most of that power. This is especially true when you are working with people who'd like to remove some – or all – of it from you. I think that there is a close relationship between:

- How you manage the boundaries around your responsibilities and your key relationships at work

and

- The degree to which you are able to preserve and use the personal power available to you in those relationships.

In this sense personal power is, in my view, neither a static nor a fluid capacity. Your experience of it will change depending on the degree to which you are able to manage your boundaries satisfactorily in key areas of your working life. Specifically I believe that it is how you manage your relationships and, in particular, how you manage the boundaries in those relationships, that dictates the degree to which you are able to experience your personal power fully in any given workplace relationship. The following example illustrates this view. It describes the relationship between three people working in the human resources department of a large engineering firm in Toulouse, France. The scenario depicts three different ways of relating to one's own personal power, to that of one's colleagues and to the boundaries in those relationships.

Example One: The Balance of Power

The human resources department is coming under increasing pressure to deliver and perform. The engineering firm is having a difficult time persuading its long-term clients to stay loyal to the company in the face of increasing competition from abroad, particularly from Germany, Japan and China. The firm needs to find ways to retain its top performing employees, to incentivize its staff and to reward excellence. The human resources department has six weeks to come up with an effective blueprint to address these challenges and sell these ideas to the Board. The Head of HR wants to undertake much of the strategic thinking around this project herself, and with workloads in the department on the rise, she promotes one of her Project Managers to manage the department's day-to-day work. This appointment will enable her to concentrate on developing the blueprint, working with her internal clients to define more closely what they will need from her department going forward and look for opportunities to develop other value-added services for them as well.

- Character One: The Head of HR is an able manager, someone who neither wants to acquire other people's power nor give away her own. She is assertive and challenging without being aggressive. She respects her own boundaries and those of her staff. She demands excellence and continued productivity from her team, and she provides them with tools, training and support when she thinks they need it. She drives herself hard, and expects that her team will also pull out all the stops when she asks them to. However, she is approachable and supportive, and defends her team from unwarranted criticism from their internal customers. She is keen that her team members should want to grow and develop their people-handling skills as ambassadors for the department.
- Character Two: The Recruitment Manager is able at his job and works long hours. He is thorough, goal oriented and low key in

style. He is quite capable of telling his team when they have fallen below the high standards he expects of them, but also listens and provides input to their work when they need him to. The Head of HR values the Recruitment Manager and he rarely hears any criticism from her. In return, the Recruitment Manager is grateful that his current boss respects his contribution to the department. He is more comfortable responding to the boundaries his manager sets in her relationship with him, and prefers to work this way rather than defining and maintaining his own boundaries with her. This is fine because he is working for a manager who isn't interested in reducing his power and who behaves in ways that safeguard it whether or not she realizes this. But it may become difficult for him should he report to a manager whose actions diminish his sense of his own personal power, whether or not they are intended to. He is disappointed to learn that he will no longer be reporting to the Head of HR, but to her newly appointed Project Manager.

- Character Three: The newly promoted Project Manager is very keen to prove herself to her new boss and her new internal clients. She has a lot to learn about how to manage her erstwhile peers, and she is starting her new role at a time of significant challenge for the whole engineering firm. She is highly goal-orientated in her approach to management, thinks in a logical way and has considerable unresolved issues around power. She is most comfortable adopting a controlling, directive approach to the people who report to her, and whenever possible, makes it clear to them that she is the one with the clout, the one in charge. She begins to dive in and out of their work, calling their key internal clients for progress reports without their knowledge. She sends e-mails to her team members pressurizing them for updates that they are not expecting to give, and wants her team to prioritize her requests for information and status reports above their ongoing client-facing work. She is abrupt, even curt, in her verbal dealings with her team members, and often sends e-mails to them rather than picking up the phone or going to someone's desk to talk to them. After a week's handover the Head of HR leaves the day-to-day management of the department to her newly promoted Project Manager, and spends all her time working on the development of the blueprint. After two weeks the newly promoted Project Manager is working over 12 hours a day. Over the next few weeks she begins to look unkempt, and starts to work the odd day from home. Her workload is huge and growing. She cannot understand how she has so much to do. She starts to look so tired that one of her colleagues asks her if she's ill.

After five weeks of reporting to his new manager, the Recruitment Manager is getting cross. He finds her management style intrusive, disrespectful and untrusting. He decides that he must meet with her to confront her apparent disrespect for the boundaries around his work, her apparent questions about his competence in his role, and the demoralizing effect that this combination of circumstances is having on his energy levels. He is worried that his new manager won't listen to him, won't take his feedback on board and consequently won't change her ways. But he decides that he has no alternative but to go ahead and meet with her. He sets up a face-to-face meeting under the title of 'Review'.

Example One: Analyzing the Political Dynamics

This is a critical juncture for the Recruitment Manager and he needs to handle the upcoming meeting well. He is used to working with a demanding but supportive boss who values him and his approach. Now he is faced with a new manager whose approach is cold, remote and pressurizing, and whose management style has created a number of interconnected issues for him, issues which affect both his relationship with his new manager and his relationship with himself. He is concerned that

- His new manager doesn't trust him to do his job, his way, to the required quality standards and on time.
- His manager's calls to his key clients, behind his back, mean that she doesn't believe in his basic competence to do his job.
- His manager's tendency to dive in and out of his work is sending a message to his key internal clients that he isn't in charge of his workload and projects – she is.
- His internal clients – never an easy bunch of people for him to deal with – will start to go to his manager with their queries instead of coming to him, and that his reputation with them will be damaged irrevocably.
- His new manager's style is undermining him, and results in him feeling that she doesn't value him or respect how he handles his responsibilities.

If he mishandles the confrontation with his new manager, the Recruitment Manager will lose further power in the relationship, and his new manager will not alter her approach to working with him at all. If he handles the confrontation well he may just succeed in influencing her to work in more productive ways not just with him but with all her managers, and be able to preserve his personal power in the process. What does he need to take into account to handle the meeting well?

- Firstly, he needs to realize that his new manager's behavior is motivated largely by a desire to acquire and retain power. Her deliberate strategy of calling her managers' internal clients without their knowledge, sending urgent requests for updates and dealing with them largely through e-mails is purposeful. It isn't the case that she is unaware of the impact of her actions on her staff. She is very aware indeed, and does it to keep her team on their toes; but it also has the effect of removing personal power from them and placing it with her own. Different members of staff will react differently to these tactics. Some will push back and confront her about her actions, others will become angry. Unfortunately for the Recruitment Manager it has the impact of reducing his energy and enthusiasm for his job, which results in him feeling cross.

- Secondly, he needs to know that his manager will not be interested in, or influenced by, hearing about how her management style annoys him and leaves him feeling mistrusted. She will not see his deteriorating energy levels as a joint problem for them to solve together. She wants to work in a unilateral way because it suits her to do so. If she wants to call one of the recruitment manager's internal clients behind his back, she will, and she won't give a second thought as to how this might undermine him.

- Thirdly, he needs to understand that his manager's behavior is a reflection of her own inner fears, fears that drive her to behave in self-destructive ways, to undermine her team members and to harm her relationships with them. Specifically she fears that she might fail in her new role, might prove incompetent at it, might not be an effective enough Project Manager to handle the workload and the learning curve she's taken on and might not have the interpersonal skills she needs to work effectively with her new team in such a challenging environment. She handles these fears in two distinct ways. Firstly she mistrusts her staff instead of herself and worries that *they* mightn't be up to *their* jobs. So she checks up on them as much as possible, calling their internal clients and demanding unplanned progress updates. Unfortunately, her behavior is counterproductive. She undermines her team members and might, in some circumstances, actually contribute to some of them becoming less effective than they would be if she didn't handle things this way. Secondly she tries to acquire and retain as much power in her managerial relationships as possible. She does this in the misguided belief that this strategy will result in her being well placed to ensure success in the department and avoid failure. It doesn't achieve these things, and in fact could directly result in some of her staff failing – and therefore, by implication, her failing too. But she uses the tactic anyway, a tactic designed to take whatever personal power she can from people who don't know how to hold on to it.

- Fourthly, he needs to recognize that his new boss has a significant need to control, and doesn't care about the consequences of using this behavior for other people. She tries to control everything her team members do, even work that she is not directly in charge of. She thinks that by controlling other people's work she will be able to influence what goes on in the department, and thereby, ensure success and avoid failure. She doesn't see the fallacy behind her excessive need to control, that the more she tries to control, the less real influence she has; that the more she tries to control the more she undermines the very people she needs to work effectively for her – her team members; that the more she tries to control, the more she gets in the way of everyone else's work and the less genuine progress can be made by her team; that the more she tries to control the more likely it will be that at least some parts of the department will perform below par – and might even fail in some instances – and that these failures to deliver will rebound on her.

Example One: Handling the Political Power Issues

The recruitment manager's strongest suit is to demonstrate to his boss just how unhelpful, and even destructive, her approach is to *her*. He needs to make an explicit link between his manager's long hours, and her consequent fatigue and her controlling approach, without suggesting that she is performing poorly, which she'd think intolerable. He would do well to address issues in his relationship with her only and avoid trying to speak for the wider department. He might want to suggest to her that

- The two of them set up a planned schedule of updates to which they both commit. If his manager wants an update outside of these regular updates, he will send her a reminder of the next scheduled update and ask her to wait until then.
- If his manager wants to speak with his key internal clients, then both of them need to be present at the meetings or conference calls. He might want to tell her that he alone is responsible for handling

his workload and that a key part of this responsibility is how he manages his relationships with his key internal clients. He would prefer that she include him in future meetings with her internal clients so that he knows what has been said and what commitments have been made. He might also say that her lengthy hours are not going to be good for her in the long term and that she needs to find a way to trust him to do the job that he has been performing perfectly competently for years.

- If his manager needs any information urgently, he will provide it for her at the earliest possible opportunity.

This approach preserves the recruitment manager's power in the relationship by placing firm boundaries around his responsibilities and her contact with him. It represents a balance between:

- Providing the new Project Manager with regular, planned updates, as well as access to the internal clients she wants to speak with, so that she feels in control and on top of things.
- Clarifying the borders around the recruitment manager's work and responsibilities so that he alone is left to get on with his duties.

However, and assuming that his manager agrees to work this way, the Recruitment Manager will have to be vigilant in reinforcing the letter of the new protocol whenever the new manager steps over the line. He can expect that she will push the boundaries every now and then just to see how far she can go, and what she can get away with. The Recruitment Manager will have to be determined and clear in his feedback every time that his boss steps over the line. This will be a considerable learning curve for him as he is more comfortable responding to his manager's boundaries in the relationship, than he is in setting them and maintaining them for himself. However, his self-esteem and reputation at work require that he learns to do this quickly, and continues to do it consistently well.

PRESERVING YOUR PERSONAL POWER AT WORK

The above example illustrates what can happen when a manager disrespects the basic boundaries around her team members' work, in a misguided attempt to gain power and feel in control. The challenge facing you if you work with such a colleague, whether or not the colleague is senior to you, is to preserve your personal power and maintain the boundaries around your work. Perhaps you'd like to take a minute to think about your own colleagues and identify which of them, if any, works in a way which erodes your personal power. You might like to answer the following questions and jot down your thoughts in the space below each one:

- Identify a colleague with whom you work whose approach to the relationship regularly results in you losing power. What does he or she do that causes you to lose power?

- How do you usually respond at these times?

- What does this response achieve for you?

- What boundaries do you need to put in place to preserve your power the next time your colleague uses this behavior with you?

- What else, if anything, would you like to say to your colleague, and when?

ORGANIZATIONAL STATUS AND RESPONSIBILITY: A DOUBLE-EDGED SWORD

So far in this chapter we have been discussing power at work solely in terms of your personal power. We have explored some of the challenges and difficulties that can be caused for you if you work with someone whose behavior erodes your personal power, and we have focused on strategies for preserving that power. Now let's move on to consider a second, but quite different, form of power at work, organizational status.

Some of you will be in a senior role and have significant organizational status. Others of you may work closely with more senior colleagues who are incumbent in a role that gives them significant organizational status. Others of you again might have sporadic access to a senior colleague with organizational status, but have access nonetheless. Being able to leverage either your own organizational status or that of a colleague can be very useful to you in getting things done, moving things along and creating the circumstances in which decisions you favor can be made or ratified. However, having organizational status also implies having significant organizational responsibility. Let's take a look at the interconnected issues of organizational status and responsibility before we move on to examine potential sources of organizational influence and how to use them effectively, whatever your position in the hierarchy.

DEFINING ORGANIZATIONAL STATUS

The term 'organizational status' might conjure up any number of words, images and phrases. Use the space below to jot down your own thoughts on this:

Take a look at what you have written and compare it with my view which is that having greater organizational status is primarily about having greater access to the means of getting things done to achieve your goals and objectives. It is no more and no less than that. It is not primarily about importance or authority, although those issues may play a part in your working experience if you have significant organizational status. The more senior you are, the greater the access you have to a range of tools for action. That's it. But there is an added complication, which is that having greater organizational status also implies having greater responsibility toward those who are affected by your decisions. Let's explore this double-edged sword in an example.

Example Two: Senior Manager

Consider the difference between the manager who:

- Recognizes that he has significant organizational status and can therefore make things happen at work; but who also feels the responsibility that this degree of organizational authority brings with it. He is acutely aware that other people are affected by his decisions – his colleagues and customers for instance – and that they will have to live with the consequences of his choices day in, day out. He realizes that he needs to make sound and responsible judgments if he is to repay the organization that employs him for its faith in promoting him to a role that carries significant organizational status. He sees his role in terms of his responsibility to get the right things done in the right way, and sees 'having power' as a tool to enable him to do these things well.
- Thinks his significant organizational status as being primarily about his own power and importance. He wants to be seen as important and keep what power he can for himself. His seniority enables him to feel that he has some stature as a person. It gives him authority over certain situations, decisions and people at work, and he likes this fact. However, he doesn't think much beyond himself and tends to make decisions on the basis of what is most comfortable for him. He knows that the consequences of his decisions and actions will inevitably be felt by other people, but nonetheless does not feel undue responsibility toward them. He sees his role mainly in terms of his own status and position, and sees 'having power' as a goal in and of itself.

Example Two: Analyzing the Political Dynamics

Let's focus on the first manager. He uses his seniority to ensure that he achieves the things he is paid to achieve. He may well have a developed political toolkit which he uses from time to time to ensure that he is able to achieve those goals associated with his role. He may well be adept at reading the political landscape, and he may well worry quite a bit about whether or not he is carrying out his role effectively. Only he will be able to judge whether the satisfaction of seeing his plans coming to fruition – at least some of the time – is worth the headache of the significant organizational responsibility he carries.

What about the second manager? The second manager wants to attain and retain power and influence simply to have it. He might fall into the trap of using his position *to meet his own personal needs* rather than to meet the requirements of his role. He might also worry less about how he is handling his responsibilities toward his staff. While 'having power' enables him to feel more substantial as a person and provides him with an ego boost, he might not pay equal attention to the responsibility toward others that comes with having significant organizational status. This manager has acquired power but has failed to take equal hold of the obligations toward others that come with organizational authority. He might not consult widely, or really listen, or consider all the options before making a decision. He might instead make decisions which are most comfortable for him, which will result in him being able to retain control, and which he can then justify afterwards if anyone asks the question, by claiming that they are about 'improved teamwork' or 'improved service' or 'a more streamlined approach' or whatever other explanation he likes. Chances are that, given his seniority, these claims will be accepted by his colleagues.

THE BENEFIT OF ORGANIZATIONAL STATUS

So how does it benefit you to have significant organizational status? It's that it will enable you to define and set the values by which the parts of the organization over which you have hierarchical influence will conduct themselves. It's as simple as that. Having organizational status means that you can shape the values by which the people who work for you go about their work, handle their customers, make their decisions, treat each other and handle their workloads. You will need to demonstrate resolve in inculcating the values that you want your staff to adopt, and you will need to mirror them scrupulously yourself if you want your staff to espouse them without cynicism. But, the bonus your organizational status will bring you is the ability to influence not only what happens in your part of the organization but also how it happens and by when.

Having explored how to maintain and preserve your personal power at work, and noted the usefulness of having significant organizational status, let's now go on to examine how to acquire and retain greater organizational influence whatever your role in the hierarchy.

USING ORGANIZATIONAL INFLUENCE TO GET THINGS DONE

You are effective at managing your boundaries and retaining your personal power when you need to be. You make sound judgments about who you can safely share information with, and who it'd be wise not to share information with. You have a suite of effective people-handling skills, and you successfully work with a wide variety of people in your workplace. Now you'd like to build on these foundations and work toward generating greater organizational influence. How do you do it? Let's take a look at how the judicious and careful use of your organizational sources of influence can help you to:

- Sponsor your ideas effectively.
- Build useful alliances.
- Retain influence.
- Promote your achievements.
- Resolve conflicts.
- Handle the political element at work effectively.

DEFINING ORGANIZATIONAL INFLUENCE

Consider the following seven potential sources of organizational influence, each of which is a potential influencing tool for use with your colleagues. Each of these influencing tools is available to people who work in organizations. As you read through them, bear in mind that, depending on your role, you might not have access to all seven tools at any time. Depending on your role and your willingness to use them, you may have access to different combinations of the tools at different times. Five of the seven sources of organizational influence are derived from research by French and Raven (1959). As you read the following descriptions consider:

- Which of the influencing tools, or which combination of them, do you use?
- Which do you never use?

We will go on to consider the application of the tools to your working life in more detail shortly. But for now it's enough for you to identify which influencing tools you prefer to use and which you avoid using all together.

- Coercive influence: This is about getting people to comply with your wishes and directives because they are afraid not to. It is about you using their fear to get them to do things for you that they wouldn't otherwise do. If you regularly or occasionally use this tool, you could do so by delivering negative consequences to a colleague, or removing positive consequences from them. The negative consequences could include you demoting someone, reducing their bonus payments, giving them dull and routine work to do, giving them an unpleasant assignment to complete, ordering them to take unfavorable holiday dates or, at worst, removing their job from them. Alternatively, you might remove positive consequences from a colleague by taking them off an assignment they enjoy and want to complete, reassigning their favored colleague to another task, repositioning their desk away from a light or quiet area into an isolating or noisy area, or telling them that their booked holiday dates are no longer available to them.

- Reward influence: This involves you influencing people to comply with your wishes because of the beneficial consequences they expect to gain by doing so. It is your ability to deliver positive consequences to colleagues, or remove negative ones from them. The positive consequences could include promotion, favorable performance appraisals, interesting work assignments, important information, opportunities to meet decision makers and senior managers or increased remuneration. Alternatively, you could remove negative consequences from a colleague by reassigning two reports who don't get on well to work on separate tasks, replacing the dull and routine side of a colleague's role with more creative and stimulating work or by offering a business trip abroad to someone qualified to do it and who likes variety and travel.

- Hierarchical influence: This is about other people complying with your wishes because of your structural position in the organization. It is, in organizational terms, the only source of influence that actually does exist, because the power to expect compliance is invested in the position you occupy or in the particular job you perform. Every manager has a degree of hierarchical influence, the degree being commensurate with their seniority. The position of manager itself holds influence and gives you authority over issues and people due to your responsibilities, and because the people you manage accept your right to direct them. They comply with your wishes because you are their manager and, whether they agree with you or not, respect that it is ultimately your call.

- Expert knowledge influence: This is influence based on your expert knowledge in your specialism, and results in other people listening to your opinion and choosing to defer to your will in that area. Expert knowledge influence is therefore based on you having a degree of skill or special knowledge which other people recognize as being authoritative and which they need to help them achieve their goals. Those of you who work in specialist organizational roles such as technology, audit, finance or HR should all be able to command a degree of expert knowledge influence with your colleagues.

- Character influence: This is influence based on your personality, your traits as a person, and the admiration and respect these afford you in the eyes of your colleagues. Your colleagues look up to you and may even want to emulate you. They chose to be influenced by you because they think that being associated with you will be good for them and their careers. In some cases colleagues might model your attitudes and behavior, and might see you as a role model. They defer to your will out of respect for you as a person.

- Information influence: This is about you being able to influence other people through having crucial pieces of organizational information, usually pieces of information that are not widely available. Your colleagues regard these pieces of information as being central to them achieving their goals, and choose to be influenced by your opinion on matters relating to them.

- Relationship influence: This is about you being able to exert organizational influence through having established relationships with your colleagues, usually more senior, powerful and well-connected people, but not necessarily so. Your influential relationships could be with your peers. These relationships result in you being included in information-giving and decision-making loops, and these connections give you kudos and prestige, as well vital knowledge about what is going on in your organization and how it affects the future direction of projects and initiatives. Your colleagues regard these connections, and the information they afford you, as being decisive and chose to defer to your will on matters relating to them.

Having defined each of the seven potential sources of organizational influence, you may now like to write down your answers to the two questions posed at the start of the section:

- Which of the power tools, or which combination of them, do you use?

```
┌─────────────────────────────────────────────┐
│                                               │
│                                               │
│                                               │
│                                               │
│                                               │
└─────────────────────────────────────────────┘
```

■ Which do you never use?

```
┌─────────────────────────────────────────────┐
│                                               │
│                                               │
│                                               │
│                                               │
│                                               │
│                                               │
└─────────────────────────────────────────────┘
```

Let's now go on to illustrate the use of these different influencing tools through two short cameos.

Cameo One: Induction Program

An effective and well regarded Production Manager works in an expanding software design company. He wants to change the way in which his team inducts and trains new members of staff. Traditionally each new member of staff is assigned to an existing production department employee and 'shadows' them for a fortnight to learn the ropes. The Production Manager thinks this an inefficient way of doing things, resulting, as it does, in the existing team member being consistently sidetracked from their work while they answer questions and explain what's what to their new colleague. He wants to handle inductions in a different way, one that doesn't reduce the effectiveness of existing employees during the induction process. His plans involve commissioning a bespoke in-house induction training program to be designed by a consultancy firm and delivered on a rolling basis by Human Resources. But he believes that, over time, the investment required to design the program will be more than returned through the speedier induction of new members of the team, and through having the existing workforce working at full capacity while new team members are inducted.

The Production Manager thinks carefully about how to approach more senior managers to gain the necessary endorsement and budget for his plans. He decides to gain support for his ideas from the Finance Director first, before setting about gaining wider support. He tells the FD that the current induction process is inefficient and costly, and provides him with estimates to justify his claim (expert influence). He then approaches the PA to the CEO to ask when the next Steering Group meeting is scheduled. The Steering Group is tasked with finding ways to improve productivity, raise standards and enhance profitability across the company. The Production Manager asks the PA to the CEO to send an e-mail to the entire Steering Group telling them that he has an item for their next agenda, before briefly outlining his proposal (expert influence). He drafts the e-mail for her and sends it to her so she can forward it to the Steering Group (relationship influence). He then attends the Steering Group meeting and describes in more detail his proposals for the in-house induction training program and the benefits this approach will have for the company. He is well thought of in the company (character influence) and his proposals are well received. The Steering Group makes a recommendation to the Board to approve the expenditure on the induction program. At the Board meeting the FD speaks in favor of the proposal (relationship influence) and the Board approves the in-house induction program.

Cameo Two: Lost Accounts

A manager in a mobile phone network is concerned at the number of long-term customers who are drifting away to other providers. The manager works in Accounts Migration, the department responsible for bringing new customers to the network from rival networks and facilitating the departure of other customers away from the network to rival companies. Her first reaction is to want to verify the figures. She tells a member of her team to double-check them (hierarchical influence) and, on finding that they are accurate, she arranges a meeting of half her team one lunchtime over sandwiches. She asks her team members why they think so many customers are leaving and flipcharts their responses. She gets a variety of answers: other networks offer cheaper call charges, promise new phones to customers as an incentive to switch to them, offer free text bundles and so on.

She decides to approach her manager with this information and two proposals of her own (expert influence). She suggests to him that while their network cannot, as yet, offer identical inducements to their customers as their competitors do, they could offer one of several other incentives instead: capped call charges for 12 months, the first 30 minutes call charges free every month or free evening and weekend calls, depending on the length of contract. Her manager, a pressured and harassed man, agrees and tells her, as he walks out of his office, that he wants to see the stats on lost customers going down. The Accounts Migration manager, knowing her boss's style of old, interprets this as an ultimatum (coercive influence) and decides that the best way to bring about a reduction in lost customers is to incentivize the customer-facing staff who handle calls from dissatisfied customers (reward influence). Over the next two days she designs a simple reward system and approaches the Customer Service Manager with it. Together they refine and improve her ideas and approach their harassed joint manager (relationship influence) with their plan. Mollified, he agrees to the small expenditure involved and, over the next few weeks, the numbers of lost accounts does reduce.

CAMEOS ONE AND TWO: ANALYZING THE POLITICAL DYNAMICS

You will notice that in several of the instances cited above the influence that a character exerts – and therefore their capacity to get things done – is synonymous with a colleague's *choice to defer to their opinion in those matters*. It is therefore imperative that the Production Manager and the Accounts Migration Manager select the right influencing tool for the right occasion, one which will genuinely hold sway with the person or people they are seeking to influence, and which will result in those people actively collaborating with them.

For instance, if the Production Manager had gone straight to the Board with his plans, and hadn't presold them to the FD and the Steering Group, he would have been relying on his reputation (character influence) and knowledge (expert influence) to be sufficient to sway the Board in favour of his plans. These two factors might have influenced the Board, but then again they might not have. Gaining the active support of the FD and the Steering Group made it much more likely that the Production Manager would get the outcome he wanted from the Board, and so maximized his potential influence in the situation.

Similarly, if the Accounts Migration Manager had responded to her manager's brusque requirement to reduce the number of lost customer accounts by ignoring it, demonstrating anger at being spoken to in that way, or with a complaint to someone else, she would have lost the opportunity to influence him to support her plans. By gaining the support of a peer, and then approaching her irascible boss in tandem with that peer (relationship influence), she cleverly diffuses his ire and influences him to support her proposed reward system.

MAXIMIZING YOUR SOURCES OF ORGANIZATIONAL INFLUENCE

Your success at maximizing your influence in your key workplace relationships revolves around your ability to select and use an effective influencing tool or combination of influencing tools, ones which really do cause your colleagues to take what you say on board, and develop or amend their thinking as a result of your input. Many times, the influencing tools you select will be the right ones for the influencing tasks at hand, but on other occasions, you may fall into the trap of selecting a tool because you are skilled at using it or because you like it. These criteria may wrong-foot you and could mean that the tool is actually the wrong one for the particular influencing job you have in mind with the particular colleague you are canvassing.

It is imperative that you practise and become efficient at using as wide a selection of influencing tools as possible. Many people only use three or four of the seven tools, and baulk at learning how to use the other three or four, preferring to continue to use their tried and tested influencing tools, even when they don't work effectively for them. Those of you who identify with this may need to address at least one of following five possible conflicts:

- You may not be skilled enough at using your preferred sources of influence. In this case you may be selecting the right tool for the right job, but may simply lack the level of aptitude you need to do the job well. You may need further development in the use of the influencing tools in question so that you can become more adept at using them.
- You may be refusing to use the very influencing tool or combination of tools you need to sway a particular colleague *on principle*. You may have made the decision not to use a particular tool or combination of tools because you observed certain of the influencing tools being used either destructively or unskilfully by other colleagues on previous occasions, and are keen to avoid repeating their mistakes. In this case, I'd urge you to take a fresh look at the potential benefits that could accrue to you once you've learned to use the tools positively and effectively, and know how to apply them well.
- You may be selecting your influencing tools on the basis of your comfort and preference at using them, not on the basis that they are the most effective choices to influence a particular colleague. In this case, you need to start selecting your influencing tools on the basis

that they will be the most effective at influencing your *colleague* rather than that they are comfortable for you to use.

■ You may only ever use a few of the available seven sources of influence and never use the rest. With some of your colleagues, this combination simply won't work and, by limiting yourself to those two or three choices only, you will not be able to have the influence you'd like no matter how skilful you are at using them.

■ You are in a situation where you are being out-influenced by a colleague who is more skilled at using their preferred sources of influence than you are at using yours. You cannot get your ideas and proposals sponsored widely among your colleagues because his or her different and contrary proposals are being supported by them instead. These ideas are being promoted by your colleague who is perceived to be more influential than you are because he or she is more skilled at using their preferred sources of influence than you are at using yours. In this case, you might need to change tack. The questions at the end of the chapter might help you to think through your options.

Having outlined the seven influencing tools, and some of the reasons why you might not be as effective at using them as you'd like, let's now apply them to a situation from your working life.

YOUR POLITICAL BEHAVIOR

Think about a possible case study from your own working life. The case study might involve a situation where you are trying to influence a colleague or colleagues to adopt a course of action you favor; or it might involve you seeking support for proposals you want to initiate. You might like to work through the following questions to help you decide how to maximize your influence over the issues and people involved. You can jot down your answers to each question in the space below it:

■ What is the situation and what outcome do you want to achieve?

■ Who are the key people you need to influence in order to bring about this outcome?

[ ]

- What actions do you want each of these people to take – or what do you want them to think – as a result of having spoken with you about the issues?

[ ]

- What views do you think each of your colleagues will have on the issues when you first speak with them?

[ ]

- Which influencing tools do you intend to use with each person?

[ ]

- During your influencing conversation, if you think that this first set of influencing tools isn't working, which alternative tools will you use with each of them instead?

[ ]

- How will you know that you have achieved the outcomes you want?

[ ]

SUMMARY AND NEXT CHAPTER

This chapter has focused on:

- The politics surrounding three forms of power at work: personal power, organizational status and organizational influence.
- Examining the nature of personal power at work, highlighting the challenges you may face when working with colleagues who don't respect the boundaries around your work and – intentionally or not – erode your personal power.
- The close relationship between organizational status and responsibility.
- Identifying seven sources of organizational influence which are available to people at work.
- Providing you with an opportunity to apply these influencing tools to your own working life.
- Illustrating how judicious and careful planning of your strategy can help you maximize the influence you could have in any given work-place situation.

The following case study builds on these themes. It focuses on what happens when two sales people win an enormous advertising account for their company, but do so by misleading their new clients about what can be achieved for them during the two weeks following their successful bid for the work. The action centres on the sales people's attempts to force their colleagues in Accounts Opening to circumvent due diligence and open the account straightaway, creating a power struggle between them and their internal supplier colleagues. The case study highlights how using influencing tools in an unskilled and destructive way has a damaging impact on working relationships between colleagues, and also adversely affects the reputation of two of them.

New Business Development

BACKGROUND AND CHARACTERS

This case study is set in an advertising company in Milan, Italy. Two salespeople, Achille and Caterina, have just won a large account for their company. The account is with a new entrant into the lucrative washing powder market, and Achille and Caterina are delighted with their success and the sales bonuses they now stand to make. They worked hard for many months to come out on top in the tender process. During their formal and informal presentations to their client's Board members they demonstrated imagination, attention to detail and, crucially, told their clients that work will start on their account immediately should they win the bid process.

Achille is good with clients, but, with his colleagues, can be patronizing. He has worked for the advertising agency for 18 months, and puts in long hours. He is very aware that the agency would not exist were it not for its sales force, and makes it clear to his colleagues in Accounts Opening and Campaign Design, whenever he deals with them, that they are primarily there, in his view, because of the efforts of people like himself. He thinks that Accounts Opening, in particular, is there to fit in with his priorities and timescales and he expects them to get accounts opened for new customers according to his instructions.

Caterina takes a different view. She thinks that Accounts Opening has a job to do, does need to follow due diligence and can't just drop everything to do as individual salespeople want. However, she also thinks the department is slow to open accounts, lacks commercial focus and is an expensive overhead given what it actually contributes to the company's bottom line. While recognizing that Achille can be unreasonable to deal with at times, she also thinks that when it comes to securing new business deals she needs him. He has an easy way with clients that she could never aspire to, and his connections and people-handling skills open doors for them that she, alone, would not be able to open. She is the more down-to-earth character and, while she would not say so to his face, she secretly enjoys it when his colleagues get a bit fed up with him. She is hardworking, is motivated to work long hours by the promise of remuneration and does want to win long-term clients and profitable business for the company.

Accounts Opening is having a hard time handling the increasingly complex accounts that the advertising company has won in recent times. Long gone are the straightforward and simple deals which could be opened in 24 hours. Now due to the intricacy and size of the deals being done, and the difficulty of getting specific details about the structure of some of the more complex aspects of those deals from members of the sales team, Accounts Opening needs at least two weeks to do its work preparatory to opening a new account of any substantial size. The department is run by Pietro, ably supported by his number two, Isabella. Isabella tends to oversee the opening of new accounts with her team of four. Both Pietro and Isabella are professional, hardworking and committed to getting the details of an account opening procedure absolutely correct. They vigorously resist any attempts by salespeople to circumvent due diligence, citing the muddles and rework created by this approach, and correctly pointing out that clients prefer to have their accounts seamlessly handled. Nonetheless more and more of their precious time is being taken up having to go over this old ground with their pushy sales colleagues who do not want to take 'no' for an answer.

SECURING THE NEW WASHING POWDER ACCOUNT

Achille and Caterina won their new account, in part, because they promised their new clients that, should their company be awarded the account, work would start straightaway on the design of a new television, magazine, newspaper and billboard advertising campaign. In effect, this would mean that the account would have to be opened straightaway so that the agency could bill for their work from day one. Achille and Caterina are well aware of the length of time it takes to open a new account, and are well aware that the Campaign Design team won't be able to start to work on the account until their clients have signed on the dotted line in, probably, two weeks time. However, when speaking with their clients, they disregard the two-week account opening period and promise them that the work will commence immediately they get the account. At the time they do this, they don't consciously think that this could be a very unwise thing to do. What they do think is that making this promise will give them the edge over their competitors in a tight tender process, and will likely secure them the business. It does give them the edge, and they do secure the business. One week after shaking hands on the deal, when the account isn't yet open and the work hasn't commenced, Achille receives a curt telephone message from his client at the washing powder company, telling him he would have expected to see some initial advertisement designs by now, and asking him where they are. Achille calls Caterina and together they go to Accounts Opening to see Isabella.

ACCOUNTS OPENING'S RESPONSE

Achille stands in her office and tells Isabella that he is unhappy that the account isn't open yet. Isabella remains calm, and seated, and reminds him of the company policy of a two-week account opening period. She points out that only one week has elapsed. Achille says he knows that, but, that in this case, it won't do. He tells her that the account must be opened immediately. He further tells her that opening the account must become top priority for her department. Isabella goes through her argument again, outlining for a second time that due diligence must be completed before an account can be opened and design work commences. She tells Achille that she is responsible for prioritizing her work and is accountable to her manager. Achille loses his temper and says, 'This just won't do! The client expects action and the client must get action'. He tells Isabella to get her finger out. He points out to her, forcibly, that he keeps her in a job, he brings in the money, and the departments which are overheads need to see things from a commercial point of view. Isabella waits until he has finished speaking and calmly but firmly tells him that 'overselling' is an unwise thing to do as it involves making false promises to clients. At this point Caterina intervenes and points out, in a reasonable tone, that the company has a lot riding on the early opening of the account, and since the client is already ringing up for progress checks, would it be possible for Accounts Opening to make an exception this one time. Isabella politely shakes her head and says it won't be. Achille raises his voice to her again and leaves her office. He walks into Pietro's office and closes the door. The two of them can be seen in animated conversation, both appearing to talk over and point at the other, until Achille leaves shouting over his shoulder that he is going to the Head of Campaign Design to see what he thinks about it.

THE OUTCOME

Over the next four days the Head of Campaign Design visits Pietro and Isabella twice and on each occasion, after a lengthy meeting, he leaves. Nothing is speeded up or slowed down as a result of these time-consuming meetings. In fact Isabella's team carry on with their work, and the account is opened on schedule 11 days after Achille and Caterina won it. Each of them receives a bonus payment for securing the deal, but not the amount either of them was expecting. During this period the client twice threatens to pull out of the deal and is only successfully prevented from doing this by the intervention of the Head of Campaign Design who takes him for dinner and outlines their preliminary plans to him. If, at this stage, the client had rejected those plans then the work that went into them would not have been paid for, the account would have gone elsewhere and the advertising company would have lost face, and would be exposed to reputational risk. These facts are made abundantly clear to Caterina and Achille by the Head of Campaign Design when he hands them their sales bonus cheques.

ANALYZING THE POLITICAL DYNAMICS: YOUR ROLE

Consider the following questions. They are designed to help you look behind the facts of the case study and examine the political dynamics at play between Achille and Caterina and their colleagues in Accounts Opening and Campaign Designs. You can jot down your answers to each question in the space below it:

- Having secured the new deal with the washing powder company, Achille takes it upon himself to order Isabella to make opening the new account top priority in her department. Which influencing tool or tools does Achille use, and how does Isabella preserve her personal power and the boundaries around her work during this dialog?

- When she intervenes in this meeting which influencing tool or tools does Caterina try and use with Isabella?

- Achille's next move is to go to Pietro's office. Which influencing tool or tools does he try to use with the Head of Accounts Opening?

> ```
>
>
>
>
> ```

- Achille then tries to enlist the active support of the Head of Campaign Design. Which influencing tool or tools does he try and use when approaching his senior colleague?

> ```
>
>
>
>
> ```

- What mistakes do Achille and Caterina make during this episode?

> ```
>
>
>
>
> ```

- What are the key lessons that Achille and Caterina would do well to take away from this episode?

> ```
>
>
>
>
> ```

LEARNING FROM ACHILLE AND CATERINA'S MISTAKES

The final section of this chapter provides a summary of the key issues that Achille and Caterina mishandle. Each of the bullet points below relates, in order, to one of the questions above. You might like to read each answer and compare it with the notes that you jotted down:

- Having secured the new deal with the washing powder company, Achille takes it upon himself to order Isabella to make opening the new account top priority in her department. Which influencing tool or tools does Achille use, and how does Isabella preserve her personal power and the boundaries around her work during this dialog?

Achille's first approach to Isabella involves him using his weight of personality and some verbal force to direct Isabella to make the opening of the new account top priority in her department. He uses a combination of coercive influence by telling her that her department is an overhead that needs to get with commercial reality; relationship influence by citing that his client is not comfortable with the slow speed of progress; and character influence by hoping that his sheer personality will hold sway with Isabella. However, he uses all of these tools unskillfully, even destructively, to try and *force* his colleague to take a course of action she does not want to take. In this respect he is not trying to influence her, he is trying to *make her* do something she is unwilling to do, something which the due diligence process by which she is bound prevents her from doing. Isabella is unmoved by all these arguments because she knows that Achille has messed up by making a false promise to his client. She doesn't feel responsible for helping him out of the muddle he has created, knowing that she has the full support of her manager Pietro. She even has the courage to point out to Achille that 'overselling is unwise', by which she means he has told his client an untruth. She preserves her personal power and the boundaries around her work under pressure from Achille by remaining calm and seated; by not allowing his emotion and aggression to affect her demeanor or alter her slow deliberate rhythm of speaking; by pointing out that it is *her* job to prioritize her work, and that she is accountable to her *manager* for meeting her priorities; and by stating the facts of the matter: that Achille is guilty of overselling, that the accounts opening procedure must be completed fully and that due diligence must be fully served as well. She does all this knowing that she has the full support of her manager, and that she is acting in accordance with company policy.

- When she intervenes in this meeting which influencing tool or tools does Caterina try and use with Isabella?

Caterina uses a very different approach with Isabella. She appeals to her reason, telling her that the company has a lot riding on the account and asks if Isabella could make an exception. Caterina doesn't use any of the influencing tools; she makes a request which is turned down.

- Achille's next gambit is to go to Pietro's office. Which influencing tool or tools does he try to use with the Head of Accounts Opening?

From the degree of heat generated by the conversation – evidenced by the two men pointing and speaking over another – it seems that

Achille has resorted again to coercive influence, and, again, fails to influence his colleague.

■ Achille then tries to enlist the active support of the Head of Campaign Design. Which influencing tool or tools does he try and use when approaching his senior colleague?

Achille hopes that the Head of Campaign Design will see things his way. He hopes that a client-facing senior manager – someone with significant organizational status – will take the same view as him, that their internal supplier colleagues in Accounts Opening are slowing them down and could potentially cost the company a new account. He hopes that the Head of Campaign Design will join him in blaming Accounts Opening for the situation he now finds himself in, and help him force them to open the account immediately. He hopes that his connection with a more senior and more influential manager will result in a degree of relationship influence which Pietro and Isabella will be unable to resist. Unfortunately for Achille, the Head of Campaign Design doesn't see it this way. He doesn't use his organizational status to compel Isabella to comply with Achille's wishes. He regards his significant position in the company as one which carries with it significant responsibility toward both his staff and his clients. He wants to do things in a way that is commensurate with his own values around respect and honesty. In fact, he has two long meetings with his colleagues from Accounts Opening, both of which seem to be conducted in an amicable manner and neither of which results in the account being opened any sooner; before bailing Achille and Caterina out by taking the new client out to dinner and successfully selling his preliminary plans to him.

■ What mistakes do Achille and Caterina make during this episode?

Achille and Caterina's first mistake is to oversell as a key part of their tender offer to their new client. Their second mistake is to assume that Accounts Opening will be able to overlook this error of judgment and will actively collude with them, without even being asked to, and open the account immediately, clearing the way for work to begin straightaway. Achille and Caterina don't, of course, see it like this. They rationalize their overselling as a legitimate sales tactic, and justify these actions to themselves by, rightly as it turns out, believing that their overselling gambit will result in them getting the account for their company. It does, but it also, in time, might have resulted in their company losing the account. It also exposes them both to significant personal reputational risk with the Head of Campaign Design. Achille and Caterina's third mistake is not to work with Accounts Opening as soon as they got the account to find out what could be done to open the new account sooner than the usual two weeks. Instead, they don't do anything. Satisfied that they have done their job and won the account, they sit back and wait, only to find out that their client becomes annoyed at the delay, putting the account in jeopardy. Then they make their fourth mistake. They visit Accounts Opening hoping to force their colleagues into circumventing due diligence and opening the account immediately. They don't listen or seek to understand the constraints their colleagues are under, and Achille, in particular, displays a lack of respect and degree of aggression that are unpleasant to deal with and unprofessional to observe. Fifthly, Achille then assumes that the Head of Campaign Design will automatically back him, and it doesn't even occur to him that he might not. In fact, the Head of Campaign Design doesn't back him at all and, after meeting with the new client, he makes it quite clear to both Achille and Caterina that he thinks that, despite their hard work, they have both handled themselves poorly. He gives them both reduced sales bonus cheques as a result. This outcome may well aggrieve both Caterina and Achille but for different reasons: Achille because he has lost income and credibility and Caterina because, while she has also lost income and credibility, more of the fault is with her colleague Achille than with her, for the way he handles Isabella, Pietro and the Head of Campaign Design.

- What are the key lessons that Achille and Caterina would do well to take away from this episode?

Achille and Caterina need to learn that true influence – with colleagues and clients – comes from using influencing tools skillfully and appropriately. Accepting that they need to bring business in, and that this is a tough and challenging role to perform, they cannot afford to do so in a way that sets up the rest of the organization – and therefore themselves – for a fall. They also need to learn that true influence comes from establishing working relationships with people that are mutually respectful. Achille, in particular, doesn't see past himself very easily and tends to think that everything that goes on around him should be for his benefit only. He doesn't factor into his thinking that he has made a promise to a client that isn't true, and that he cannot automatically assume that his colleagues will go along with it and cover up for him. Achille uses a number of the influencing tools so ineffectively that they become rods for his own back. He would do well to learn how to handle them effectively and build influential relationships with those people who work with him, so that the next time he needs support from his colleagues, he will stand a chance of being able secure it. Caterina would do well to learn that she needs to distance herself, verbally and clearly, from some of Achille's more aggressive behavior, or else she runs the risk of being seen as being as politically unsound as him.

This case study has focused on the pitfalls on using influencing tools unskillfully to try and force colleagues to comply with your will. It has demonstrated how misuse of these influencing tools can injure your reputation, lose you the respect of senior managers and cause clients to become dissatisfied with your work. The case study has examined how one initial misjudgment can escalate out of control if the people trying to resolve the issues do so without a set of effective influencing skills, without respect for the boundaries around their colleague's work, and without taking into account the values differences between themselves and those colleagues. It also highlighted the impact that one senior manager can have on a situation when he wants to use his organizational status to reinforce values around honesty and respect.

The following chapter will build on these themes and examine a set of issues which affect every single workplace relationship that you are involved in, trust. It examines the issue of trustworthiness in your colleagues and identifies how to tell the difference between trusting and untrusting behavior at work.

Objective Criteria for Assessing Trusting Behavior

The preceding four chapters have focused on how to get things done productively with other people and, crucially, how to take into account the political realities of the situations you find yourself working in. The previous two sets of tools and case studies focused on how to work effectively with others to achieve your goals and on the pitfalls of failing to consider the consequences of your actions for your business relationships, your colleagues, your clients and, ultimately, yourself. Let's now move on to discuss an issue central to the quality of every business relationship you have in your workplace, the level of trust that exists between you and the people you are working with. This chapter will explore the three interconnected issues of:

- The degree to which a colleague – or you – uses trusting or untrusting behavior at work.
- Your particular way of judging a colleague to be trustworthy or untrustworthy.
- How you decide whether a colleague's behavior is politically motivated.

In this chapter we are going to explore the complex set of factors that influence your decisions to trust or not to trust the key colleagues that you work with day in, day out. The chapter will help you to:

- Think through what 'trust at work' means to you.
- Examine a series of factors that might lead you to decide whether any particular colleague is worthy of your trust or not worthy of your trust.
- Introduce you to a set of objective criteria for determining what constitutes trusting behavior, as opposed to untrusting behavior.
- Evaluate your own behavior, and that of a key workplace contact, in the light of those criteria.

This chapter has three key objectives. The first aim is to help you understand your own actions and to guide you in evaluating to what degree you use trusting or untrusting behavior with your different colleagues and workplace contacts. The second aim is to enable you to make sound judgments about the trusting or untrusting behavior you observe in your colleagues. The third and final aim is to develop your understanding of how those sound judgments can allow you not only to work with the varied levels of trusting and untrusting behaviors you find in the workplace, but to keep whatever political motivations your colleagues may have in their proper perspective.

TRUSTING BEHAVIOR OR TRUSTWORTHY CHARACTER?

Before we go any further, let's make an immediate distinction between the degree to which a colleague – or you – might use trusting or untrusting *behavior* and the degree to which they might be trustworthy or untrustworthy *as a person*.

For most people, the two things go hand in hand. A person who demonstrates trust in their behavior toward others probably does so because they are trustworthy themselves. Likewise, people who use untrusting behavior usually turn out to be untrustworthy. It might, however, be a good idea to pay particular attention when making these links. Although they may seem logical as ideas, in practice they don't always automatically follow. It isn't always possible to form a view about someone's trustworthiness based solely on observations about how they operate in their job or how they treat you. To make an accurate interpretation of their behavior you need to exercise wise judgment, and take into account how they handle a wide range of people, including yourself, and the other people they work with.

In addition, you really need to get to know someone well as a colleague before finally deciding if they are worthy of credibility. While their behavior might be comfortable and straightforward to deal with, it doesn't automatically follow that their underlying intentions are equally transparent. There are times when trusting behavior is nothing more than a person's basic default mode. Some workplace contacts are capable of presenting themselves as fully open and honest, thereby lulling you into a false sense of security. Their motivations, however, might not be in any way straightforward.

THE DECISION TO TRUST

The decision to trust is a very personal one and you will have your own criteria for deciding whether or not to trust a colleague. Some of you will start off trusting your workplace contacts and only change your stance when presented with evidence of behavior that you consider to be untrustworthy. Others of you will play it the opposite way round. You will start off being more guarded and extend trust to colleagues only as you experience behavior which engenders more leniency on your part. There are many possible permutations in between as well. To add a further level of complexity some of you will adopt a different approach with different people, perhaps choosing one approach with people with whom you work closely such as your team members, while choosing a different approach with people who have more seniority than you such as your senior managers, or who are contacts external to your employer such as clients. There are no rights and wrongs, only individual preferences. However, the more insight you have into the basis upon which you make your preferences, and the more aware you are of your values around trust, the more choice you will have about whom to trust, to what degree and over which issues.

This chapter will introduce you to a set of objective criteria which you can use to help you assess the extent to which a particular workplace contact's behavior is trusting or untrusting. You can use these criteria at any stage of a workplace relationship provided that you have some actual experience of the person's behavior against which to judge. In conjunction with the tools we've already examined, these criteria will help you to distinguish between behavior which:

- While untrusting and therefore difficult to deal with, is not actually untrustworthy per se, but is more a reflection of the person's tricky role or position in the organization.
- Is a signal that the person's intent is not reliable and constant, and that they might be untrustworthy.

This distinction is important in our discussion about political behavior, how to work with it effectively and handle it well. You will need to make accurate judgment calls about which of your colleagues is inherently untrustworthy and therefore could be political in their intent; which are untrusting and challenging to work with but likely to be nonpolitical; and which are trusting and trustworthy, and likely to be reliable and effective coworkers. Consider the following example which illustrates this key distinction.

Example One: Mixed Messages

An Art History teacher starts work at her new school and, on her first day during mid-morning coffee, meets the school Principal. He tells her that her third-year course, Introduction to Art History, is over-subscribed and that she will have to begin turning students away. She responds by saying that, if the demand is there, perhaps she could offer the same class twice in one week to cater for everyone who wants to attend. The Principal smiles, says 'good idea, let's do it' and moves away to speak with someone else. The Art History teacher decides to act straightaway and, after checking her weekly teaching rota, advertises a second third-year Introduction to Art History class on a Friday afternoon. Several days later she is dismayed to find out that the Head of the Art Department has refused her permission to run the extra class following a meeting he has had with the Principal. The Art History teacher forms the view that the Principal has gone back on his word. She arranges to see him and asks him why he has changed his mind:

- In his subsequent reply the Principal acknowledges that she must be disappointed but is also quite evasive. He comments that it'd be best to wait and see how many students actually attend the first class before arranging any further classes. The Art History teacher is confused, and asks for clarification about what situation the Principal is trying to prevent. The Principal doesn't expand on his original answer but tells the Art History teacher that it'd be better for her to walk before she decides to run. The Art History teacher is perplexed and disappointed at the tone and ambiguity of the Principal's comments. She realizes that the meeting has drawn to an end and leaves the room feeling decidedly uncomfortable. However, she complies with his wishes and removes her advertisement for the Friday afternoon Introduction to Art History class.
- The Principal says he hasn't changed his mind. The Art History teacher reminds him of the conversation they had over coffee, when she suggested running the Introduction to Art History class twice in one week to accommodate all the third-year students who expressed an interest in attending. The Principal doesn't reply. He smiles slightly and asks her 'what point are you trying to make?' The Art History teacher realizes that she is getting into deep water, but decides to press on anyway. She says that, at the time, she took his comment to mean that she had the green light to run the course twice in one week. The Principal smiles again. He stands up

from behind his desk, waits for the Art History teacher to do like-wise and, while guiding her by the elbow toward the closed door to his office, tells her that everything is open to interpretation. He opens the door for her, waits for her to leave and closes the door behind her.

Example One: Analyzing the Political Dynamics

Let's consider what has happened in these two scenarios, starting with the first one. The Principal in this scenario is not politically motivated in this instance and is not inherently untrustworthy either. But he is still difficult to deal with, and lacks any transparency in his dealings with the Art History teacher over his decision to take a u-turn on the second class. He:

- Initially tells her that she can go ahead and run the Introduction to Art History class twice a week for third-year students.
- Meets with the Head of the Art Department and changes his mind.
- Tells the Head of Art to inform the Art History teacher of this change of direction, but does not follow-up to make sure that his message has been conveyed.
- Fails to explain his volte-face to the Art History teacher when given an opportunity to do so.
- Is shifty and hard to pin down in his meeting with her.
- Leaves her feeling that, while he hasn't exactly lied to her, he has been less than open, and more than a little slippery, in his dealings with her.

The questions which his behavior raises for the Art History teacher are more to do with what he leaves unsaid than what he actually does say. He offers her no explanation, rationale or context for his change of heart. He does acknowledge that she must be disappointed, thereby accepting that a change of decision on his part has occurred. But he doesn't handle the meeting well, partly because he lacks the interpersonal skills to do so and also because he is caught in the middle of a conflict himself. On the one hand he:

- Does want to schedule the second class.
- Sees this as a way to incentivize and encourage a new member of staff.
- Agrees with the logic of giving students the opportunities they want, even if this means providing more classes than originally scheduled.

On the other hand, in making the decision to offer a second third-year class without discussing the idea with the Head of the Art Department, the Principal has placed himself in a tricky position. He has inadvertently undermined the authority of his Departmental Head and, when this is forcibly pointed out to him a few days later, he has no option but to back down and take a u-turn. However, he cannot tell the Art History teacher that this is what has happened, without losing face and undermining his own position. So he is vague and elusive with her and hopes that she will get the message. His conduct is difficult to deal with but he is not an untrustworthy man, more someone caught in the cross fire of politics of his own making.

In the second instance the Principal is acting politically throughout, and he is deeply untrustworthy as well. He:

- Lets the Art History teacher think she has his permission to put on the second class on a Friday afternoon.
- Has no real intention at any stage of allowing the class to proceed.
- Subsequently meets with the Head of the Art Department to tell him that the Art History teacher has overstepped the mark and is putting on an additional unsanctioned class, a class he expects the Head of Art to put a stop to.
- Uses the subsequent meeting with the Art History teacher to make it clear to her that he is the one with the power; and that he is free to change his mind, alter his decisions and do what he likes whether or not it is what she expects, thought she had agreed to or wants to happen.
- Is patronizing and superior with her, unilaterally ending the meeting when he wants to, without resolving her issues or addressing any of the points she puts to him.
- Leaves her feeling that he has handled this episode in a way that is arbitrary and ambiguous, and that what he says at any one time is likely to be expedient and could be inconsistent with what he subsequently does.

The questions his behavior raises with the Art History teacher are more to do with how he behaves than what he says. He doesn't answer the points she puts to him, but smiles condescendingly instead. This changes the conversation from one in which they are both active, equal participants to one where he has the upper hand. He replies to her key point that he had apparently given her permission to go ahead with a second class with a question instead of an answer. The question itself – 'what point are you trying to make?' – is a clear red flag, warning the Art History teacher not to question his judgment, conduct or influence. When she fails to back down sufficiently, he reinforces his authority by escorting her out of his office.

The Principal acts throughout his dealings with the Art History teacher in a political and untrustworthy way. He says one thing but does another purely to wrong-foot his new employee, show her who is boss and make sure that she realizes that he and he alone has ultimate influence in the school. He also shows her that he can be underhand and lacks transparency. The Art History teacher is left in no doubt at all about who is in charge. She will also doubt the integrity of her Head of Department from now on, as she will be unsure what role he has played behind the scenes. These manipulations of his staff members serve the interests of the Principal because they keep everyone who works for him wrong-footed and off balance. This inhibits them and gives him the opportunity to capitalize on their uncertainty. His tactics ensure that he gains and retains power and control by:

- Demonstrating to his teachers and departmental heads that he has total authority in matters he chooses to influence, even though he has little integrity and cannot be trusted.
- Leaving his staff members unsure of the trustworthiness of their coworkers, thus precluding colleagues from forming alliances and working closely with one another as they can never be sure who among them is trustworthy and who is not.
- Preventing any groups of staff from working together to gain influence and, as he sees it, power which may collectively prove greater than his.

This Principal is both untrustworthy and political in his dealings with his staff and makes this agenda crystal clear from day one of his new Art History recruit's employment.

What is interesting is that, in both cases, the Principal uses untrusting behavior; he doesn't address points that are put to him, he is closed and guarded in his replies and he lacks openness. However, in only one of the two cases are these behaviors signals of an untrustworthy and political mind.

WHAT DOES TRUST AT WORK MEAN TO YOU?

The second Principal exhibits a degree of untrustworthiness that, fortunately, you'd be unlucky to encounter at work. The degree of challenge associated with his behavior is compounded by the fact that he has significant organizational authority, being the person in charge of the school. Hopefully, you won't have to deal with a colleague as duplicitous as him, or as skilled at playing coworkers off against one another as he proves to be. So what are your experiences of working with colleagues whom you regard as trustworthy, who have proven themselves to be untrustworthy or who you fear might be untrustworthy? Let's find out by turning our attention to examine what trust means to you in your day-to-day work.

Consider what the word 'trust' means to you in the context of your workplace relationships. You can use the space below to jot down the words and phrases that come to mind:

```
```

Another question to consider is, to what extent does having 'trusting working relationships' matter to you? Again you might like to jot down any thoughts or conclusions you have in relation to this question in the space below:

```
```

Some of you might think that trust is vital to any working relationship and that without it you are less likely to:

- Work well with your colleagues.
- Think creatively.
- Work collaboratively.
- Solve joint problems effectively.

Others of you – particularly those of you who regularly work in cultures where there is little trust or who work in relationships which are adversarial – may well say that it is quite possible to work productively with people day in, day out even if there is little or no trust between you. Your experience may be that to get things done you have to work in specific ways designed to protect you while facilitating progress. These might include:

- Using information judiciously.
- Being guarded about who you share your plans with.
- Being thoughtful and considerate about how you go about getting things done.

However, you may still believe that it is perfectly possible to work effectively without that much trust.

So what is trust and why do people choose to trust some colleagues but choose not to trust others?

DEFINING TRUST AT WORK

Ultimately trust is a choice based on evidence of behavior that you have observed or experienced often enough to have faith in. It is one of the ultimate judgment calls at work. The following definitions of what trust is and is not are adapted from Mayer et al. (1995). Trusting a colleague does not mean that you:

- Think they are infallible and will never make an honest mistake.
- Have absolute confidence in what they do, what they say and how they say it.
- Agree with every view, opinion or statement they offer.
- Can forecast how they will approach every single situation they are involved in at work.

So if trust isn't about these four things, what is it about? To trust a colleague means that, for the greater part, you think that the colleague you trust is likely to:

- Handle things in ways that you can work with.
- Conduct themselves with sufficient integrity that you'll feel comfortable working with them.
- Work consistently toward the goals and objectives associated with their role or roles.

Trusting a colleague is therefore an individual choice based on evidence that you consider credible and which you believe to be, by and large, predictive of future conduct.

Some of you may make rapid, instinctual decisions about who is or is not trustworthy. For you the evidence you believe is your instinct about your colleague. Others of you may take your time and want to see repeated behavioral evidence of a person's values before you determine whether or not to trust them, and over which issues to trust them as well. Some colleagues will prove trustworthy in some areas of their working lives, but not in others, and your job is to make accurate distinctions about where these boundaries lie.

DECIDING WHOM TO TRUST

So how can you tell the wood from the trees? The following four criteria can help you assess the degree to which you regard any particular colleague as being trustworthy. The criteria are adapted from research by Drucker (1997) and Sinetar (1988).

Typically, in order to trust a colleague, you are likely to want to see evidence that he or she will consistently demonstrate:

- Integrity: By doing what they say they will do, by when they say they will do it, and by acting in accordance with their stated beliefs.
- Reliability: By faithfully keeping their commitments and promises to you and, if they cannot do so, informing you at the earliest possible opportunity.
- Goodwill toward you: By respecting and honoring you and their relationship with you.
- Dependability: By exhibiting behavior which is, by and large, constant and steady.

You might like to identify a workplace relationship with a colleague whom you consider to be trustworthy, and review their behavior in the light of these criteria. You may want to jot down your responses to the following five questions in the spaces below them:

- To what extent does your colleague demonstrate integrity by consistently doing what they say they will do by when they say they will do it?

- To what extent does your colleague demonstrate reliability by working faithfully toward their commitments and promises?

> [blank box]

■ To what extent does your colleague demonstrate goodwill toward you by respecting their relationship with you?

> [blank box]

■ To what extent does your colleague demonstrate predictability by exhibiting behavior which is, by and large, constant and dependable?

> [blank box]

■ Given your responses to the four questions above, what overall conclusion have you come to about the trustworthiness of your colleague?

> [blank box]

POLITICS: THE EROSION OF TRUST

Political behavior at work erodes trust. It's as simple as that. You only need to observe or experience a colleague using a truly political behavior once to learn that:

■ they are likely to do so again
■ you are dealing with someone who is out for themselves
■ they are willing to use tactics that are unpleasant to deal with

- they are potentially destructive to their working relationships
- they don't value or want to preserve your trust.

Not valuing trust means that they are unlikely to go out of their way to safeguard it, and won't regret acting in ways that could injure their working relationship with you and erode any trust: you offer them. Working with a trustworthy colleague is straightforward. It's working with those people who are untrustworthy, those whose trustworthiness is not proven, or those who you suspect might prove untrustworthy in the future that is likely to take up your headspace and concern you.

Let me remind you of the distinction made at the start of the chapter. It is between behavior which:

- While untrusting and therefore difficult to deal with, is not actually untrustworthy per se, but is more a reflection of the person's tricky role or position in the organization.
- Is a signal that the person's intent is not reliable and constant, and that they might be untrustworthy.

Accurately identifying which category a particular behavior belongs to is important in determining how you subsequently handle the difficulties it creates for you. For instance, where a colleagues' behavior is opaque but isn't inherently untrustworthy or politically motivated you may chose to handle the relationship differently from a colleague who is clearly using behavior which is both untrustworthy and political. Getting this judgment call right is vital, and having objective criteria to help you do so can make all the difference between making the wrong call and making the right one. While you might not be able to get these judgments right all the time, you can eliminate some of the doubt by determining whether a colleague or contact's conduct is consistent with trusting behavior or untrusting behavior. You might later find evidence to change your view, but it is, at least initially, reasonable to work on the basis that a colleague who uses trusting behavior with you is quite likely to be trustworthy in the long run; and, until you have evidence to the contrary, it is reasonable to work on the basis that a colleague who uses untrusting behavior with you might well prove be untrustworthy in the long run.

So let's now examine a set of objective criteria which will help you make a valid assessment about the degree to which a colleague is using behavior that is trusting or untrusting. These criteria are adapted from research by Libove and Russo (1997).

FOUR CRITERIA FOR ASSESSING BEHAVIOR

Start by selecting a colleague or workplace contact, perhaps someone with whom you have a more difficult, rather than less difficult, relationship. You might like to evaluate that person's behavior using the four criteria below. They will help you to assess the degree to which your colleague or contact uses *trusting behavior* or *untrusting behavior* in their relationship with you. Take note of the words in italics. You are not evaluating their trustworthiness in relation to you or their political intentions in relation to certain issues. You are only evaluating the degree to which they use *trusting* or *untrusting behavior*.

You will see that each of the four criteria below is presented as a pair of contrasting descriptions. In each case there is a description of a trusting behavior followed by a description of an untrusting behavior. Start by reading each pair of descriptions and decide whether the colleague or contact you have chosen tends to use trusting behaviors with you, or untrusting behaviors or bits of both. You might like to write down your conclusions in the space below each pair of descriptions:

Criteria 1: Monitoring Your Actions
Trusting Behavior: When working with you, your colleague is quite willing to let you make decisions unilaterally, even decisions which affect them as well as you. They are willing to give you the freedom to initiate and act on their behalf without their prior say-so. They also allow you to make commitments on their behalf as well. In fact, in most circumstances, they afford you the freedom to act and decide as your judgment dictates.

Untrusting Behavior: When working with you, your colleague relies on rules, policies, procedures and service level agreements to get things done. They enforce these regulations and levels of approval and they see their role as being, partly at least, to monitor and control your behavior to make sure that you comply with the agreed regulations.

Criteria 2: Evidence of Goodwill

Trusting Behavior: When working with you, your colleague regularly demonstrates goodwill toward you. They willingly share their ideas, time and opinions with you. They also freely share with you any information they have that they think you'd benefit from knowing, might like to know or might need to know. They do so without expecting to get anything back in return.

Untrusting Behavior: When working with you, your colleague sticks to formal obligations and only meets up with you when they have to. If they do decide to give you anything potentially useful – ideas, time, opinions or information – they only do so in the expectation that they'll get something useful in return.

Criteria 3: Evidence of Openness Toward You

Trusting Behavior: When working with you, your colleague gives you unrestricted access to their business contacts and database. They also openly share information and their ideas with you, even information which paints them in an unfavorable light. They have few secrets from you, and make sure that they address fully any issues that you put to them.

Untrusting Behavior: When working with you, your colleague only shares limited information with you and, sometimes, doesn't share any information at all. They may prevent you from accessing their files, database or contacts lists. They may not share much with you, might fail to address points you put to them or only partially answer your points. They may hide their real views and opinions from you out of fear that you might use the information against them.

Criteria 4: Evidence of Risk-Taking with You

Trusting Behavior: When working with you, your colleague readily shares information with you which, if you misused it, would place them at risk. They also share information with you which paints them in a disadvantageous light, comfortable in the belief that you won't take advantage of them for doing so. They give you the room to make decisions and commitments on their behalf.

Untrusting Behavior: When working with you, your colleague withholds information from you to make sure that they retain the upper hand. They check up on you to ensure that you have followed through on the commitments that you've made to them. Before they allow you to do anything on their behalf, they agree with you the steps you will take, and monitor your activity afterwards making sure that you did take those steps and those steps only.

Having used the four criteria to assess the degree to which your colleague uses trusting or untrusting behavior, consider what conclusions you can come to about their trustworthiness and how politically minded they are. You might like to answer the following questions to help you do this, jotting down your answer to each question in the space below it:

- Having made an assessment about the degree to which your colleague uses trusting or untrusting behavior, what opinion have you formed about their overall trustworthiness?

- Having made an assessment about the degree to which your colleague uses trusting or untrusting behavior, what opinion have you formed about how politically minded they are?

[blank box]

- In what ways, if any, will you alter your behavior with them as a result of these conclusions?

[blank box]

- What is your aim in making these alterations to your behavior?

[blank box]

YOUR POLITICAL BEHAVIOR

I firmly believe that the starting point for handling other people well is to know yourself well. Consider the four criteria for assessing trusting or untrusting behavior again but this time with your own conduct in mind. Choose a workplace relationship – any one – at random and evaluate your conduct in it using the four criteria. You could re-read the descriptions above with your own behavior in mind and then, in the context of the working relationship you've chosen, write down in the spaces below your conclusions about whether you consider your own behavior with this person to be trusting, untrusting or a mixture of both on each of the four criteria:

Criteria 1: Monitoring Your Contact's Actions

[blank box]

Criteria 2: Evidence of Your Goodwill Toward Your Contact

```



```

Criteria 3: Evidence of Openness with Your Contact

```



```

Criteria 4: Evidence of Risk-Taking with Your Contact

```



```

SUMMARY AND NEXT CHAPTER

This chapter has highlighted that

- The links between trusting or untrusting behavior, trustworthiness or untrustworthiness and political intentions are sometimes difficult to pinpoint accurately.
- Trusting behavior alone isn't a reliable indicator of whether or not a colleague is a trustworthy character, but it's a good starting point.
- Some untrusting behavior may not be a signal that the colleague using it is inherently untrustworthy or politically minded – they may simply be in a tricky political situation.
- The decision to trust is a very personal one, and that each of you will have your own criteria for deciding whom to trust and over what.

The chapter identified a number of criteria that you can use when assessing whether or not to trust a workplace contact. It also examined how easily trust can be eroded when your colleagues – or you – use political behavior at work, and outlined four clear objective criteria for assessing the degree to which a workplace contact's behavior is more or less trusting. The chapter ended with an opportunity for you to apply these criteria to a colleague's behavior with you and to your own behavior with a colleague.

The following case study builds on these themes. It focuses on what happens when a high-performing young manager is threatened with a poor appraisal rating by her boss who she had previously thought of as a business friend. The boss lets her personal agenda influence her assessment of her report's performance and uses the appraisal meeting to undermine her, destroying the trust which the young manager had thought existed between them.

Appraisal

BACKGROUND AND CHARACTERS

This case study is set in Tokyo in the music industry. It focuses on two American employees of a large music group who work to upgrade and install the complex technology that supports the Tokyo music production unit. Their work takes in sites across the Far East and Asia. A senior and influential manager, Stephanie, is conducting the yearly performance evaluation of her top performing young manager, Bryony. Bryony has reported to Stephanie since she joined the music group just under two years ago. While the two women have very different styles and value systems, they get on well enough that Bryony considers them to be friends, albeit business friends. Stephanie and Bryony both travel extensively – but usually separately – and when they are in the Tokyo office at the same time they go for the occasional drink after work. They sometimes get a sandwich together at lunchtime and they share an interest in tennis. Last year Stephanie used her contacts to get VIP tickets for Bryony and her partner to attend the US Open Men's Singles Final at Flushing Meadow.

Bryony is a loyal character, hard working, ambitious, talented, confident and self-reliant. She isn't a devious thinker, nor is she politically minded. Her influence and growing reputation come from her interpersonal skills and her ability to work effectively with a wide range of colleagues. She seems to have no trouble establishing rapport with people and gets top performances out of most of those who report to her. Due to her own work ethic and endeavor she has had a great year. She spent little time in the Tokyo office during the year as her schedule took her to various locations in the Far East and Asia. Throughout her travels she was in contact with her boss Stephanie through e-mail and voicemail, updating her on progress, outlining what she had achieved and had yet to accomplish on her different projects and highlighting for her upcoming issues that Stephanie might want to think through. During the year Bryony managed significant upturns in the performance of the technology installation teams in both the Hong Kong and Singapore offices; oversaw the design and installation of an effective, custom-made mainframe system in Tokyo and reduced costs in three out of the four teams she directly manages. She also received excellent feedback from key internal clients according to an externally managed Client Satisfaction Survey that the music group commissioned. By anyone's standards Bryony has had a terrific year.

Stephanie has been with the group for over 20 years. She is ambitious, a bit lazy, wears expensive designer suits, always travels business class and is a competitive and, at times, manipulative member of the workforce. She is also very clever and quite capable of breaking the odd rule or two without being found out. Stephanie uses her role and seniority to make sure that departmental meetings she attends happen to a schedule that suits her, and isn't above canceling or rescheduling a meeting with any of her junior colleagues should her lunch run over or simply because she wants to do something else. Lacking discipline and respect for others, she regularly fails to attend meetings she has arranged and sees nothing wrong in expecting everyone else to fit in with her timescales as and when she chooses. Stephanie thinks Bryony is a very useful person to have on her team. She sees her as someone who works very hard, gets results, doesn't need managing or monitoring, and who is capable of giving tough messages to her team. However, Stephanie also thinks that Bryony is potentially too big for her boots, might get too influential and might not want to do things in the somewhat shady way that Stephanie prefers. She worries that if Bryony gets any more senior, or gets the ear of any managers who are more senior or more influential than Stephanie, then she, Stephanie, might lose some of the privileges that her current working arrangements bring her.

THE TRUST ISSUES

Bryony is a naturally trusting character. She uses trusting behavior herself – with everyone – and isn't naturally judgmental or suspicious of anyone. In fact, while she is well aware that Stephanie sometimes sails close to the wind, her natural reaction is to shrug her shoulders and say to herself, 'that's just her way'. However, she draws the line absolutely at being involved in anything shady herself, as it would go against her value system and ways of working. Bryony knows that Stephanie isn't always ethical in her approach. She knows Stephanie will take credit for other people's work if she thinks it's in her interests to do so, and is well aware that Stephanie isn't above lying, threatening, distorting facts and being evasive in her dealings with other people if she deems it advantageous to adopt this approach. Despite all this Bryony still doesn't mistrust her. She regards these features of Stephanie's conduct as examples of the style differences between them, and doesn't interpret them as evidence of her being a potentially or actually untrustworthy character. Being naturally averse to judging others and being nonpolitical herself, she doesn't form a view about whether her manager's behavior is or isn't political, preferring to perceive her as someone who does things differently to her. She remains open to her manager, and sees her as someone who has bags of experience and contacts, and as someone from whom she can learn a lot.

Stephanie doesn't trust anyone, ever, and only uses mistrusting behavior. She thinks that people who trust their colleagues are worthy of her contempt – although she is careful not to reveal this point of view at work. She is naturally guarded and speaks in as few words as possible. She uses information carefully to ensure that the person she is talking to realizes that she is often in the know, and accordingly should be treated with respect. She uses untrusting behavior all the time. She is rarely open, doesn't talk about herself, gives time reluctantly to people when she has to but, otherwise, deals with people strictly on a need to know basis, and only when she chooses to. She is capable of making her feelings very clear when she thinks someone has let her down, and usually makes sure that everyone else knows about it too. She enjoys having one over on her colleagues and regularly keeps her ear to the ground for information that she can use against people in the future. Stephanie regards herself as an operator, someone adept at manipulating both her colleagues and the group's internal systems, and she thoroughly enjoys the kudos and satisfaction that this way of doing things brings her. She thinks that Bryony is both naïve and vulnerable, and she intends to exploit both for her own ends. She is aware that Bryony trusts her and thinks that this is a chink in her armor which could prove ultimately useful to her, Stephanie.

THE WEEK BEFORE THE PERFORMANCE EVALUATION MEETING

With her performance evaluation meeting coming up Bryony decides to produce a list of her achievements which she intends to take to the meeting with Stephanie. Both of them have completed lengthy documentation as part of the performance evaluation process, but only Stephanie has had access to both documents. Bryony's list of achievements is impressive, testament to both her effort and her skill at managing a huge workload effectively. Stephanie is traveling for most of the week leading up to the performance evaluation meeting, so Bryony is unable to test the water with her about what overall rating she might expect to get. Bryony's next promotion will be directly linked to this performance evaluation rating. She is expecting top ranking on the group's performance rating system, and is quietly confident that the salary raise she expects on receiving her promotion will reflect her value to the group and to her manager.

THE MORNING OF THE PERFORMANCE EVALUATION MEETING

The performance evaluation meeting is scheduled for 0930. Bryony arrives in the office at 0810 and is disconcerted to notice that Stephanie, who usually arrives before her, isn't in her office. She asks around and is told that Stephanie called in to say that she will be late, but didn't say by when she would arrive. At 0930 Stephanie still hasn't arrived so Bryony calls her cell phone, which is switched off.

THE PERFORMANCE EVALUATION MEETING

The performance evaluation meeting commences at 1500 after being put back twice by Stephanie. Stephanie eventually arrives at her desk at 1130, and offers no explanation or rationale to Bryony for why she is late. She doesn't acknowledge that she has missed the scheduled 0930 performance evaluation meeting, but asks her PA to e-mail Bryony and inform her that the time of the meeting has been put back to 1330. She then puts it back again to 1445, before eventually arriving at 1500. The meeting begins with Bryony both frustrated and annoyed, and with Stephanie saying that she will have to keep it short because she is due elsewhere in 20 minutes.

Stephanie asks Bryony, 'So, how do you think you've done this year?' but in a frosty and flat tone. Bryony is thrown and, having taken a minute to think, says 'Is that a joke?' with an uncomfortable laugh. She can't really believe that Stephanie needs to ask whether or not she thinks she's had a good year. She wonders if Stephanie is ill, or whether some emergency has detained her that morning and has upset her. But Stephanie's cold and wintry demeanor doesn't invite the question so Bryony waits for her manager to reply. She is amazed when Stephanie, in the same icy tone, asks her again 'So, you think you've had a good year?' Bryony produces the sheet that she wrote outlining her achievements. She holds it out to Stephanie and tells her that she's had a great year and here is the proof. Stephanie ignores the sheet and says 'So, you think it's all about performance?' Bryony simply doesn't know what to say for a minute. Having recovered her composure she says 'Of course it's about performance, it's my performance evaluation'. Stephanie counters by saying 'It is never about performance alone, but always about performance and conduct ... performance and *trustworthiness*'. She lingers over the word to give it added emphasis.

Bryony asks what she has done to be untrustworthy, which is what she thinks is being implied by her manager. Stephanie tells her that there are certain things she would like to tell Bryony but cannot, because she cannot trust her. Bryony is floored and searches her mind for clues as to what Stephanie is alluding to, what instances she is referring to where she has acted in an untrustworthy manner. Finding none, she says that she has the right to a performance evaluation on her performance record.

This produces the explosive reply from her boss, 'Are you questioning my judgment?' Bryony says 'Of course not. But I don't know where this is going either', to which Stephanie replies, 'I'll give you a choice then. I can appraise you now, but I don't think you'd be happy with the result. Or you can go away, think about what I've said and come back and see me in a few days when you've had time to reflect. Maybe then we can have a meaningful and fruitful discussion'. She pauses for effect. Receiving no answer from a bewildered Bryony Stephanie gets up and walks out of the room, leaving her colleague sitting dazed and confused. Bryony has no idea why she is being treated like this, but is very clear that her boss has just revealed her true nature to her. She is also aware that their relationship has become adversarial overnight, and that it is one in which Stephanie holds the upper hand.

ANALYZING THE POLITICAL DYNAMICS: YOUR ROLE

Consider the following questions. They are designed to help you look behind the facts of the case study and examine the political dynamics at play between Stephanie and Bryony. You can jot down your answers to each question in the space below it. The questions invite you to analyze the political dynamics from Bryony's point of view:

- Up until her performance evaluation meeting Bryony consistently extends trust to Stephanie despite evidence that her manager's conduct isn't worthy of trust. What behavioral evidence does Bryony foolishly ignore?

```

```

- Bryony also fails to recognize Stephanie's behavior as untrusting and untrustworthy, preferring to interpret it as idiosyncratic rather than duplicitous. What behavioral evidence does she overlook in assessing her manager's character?

```

```

- Why do you think Bryony finds it so difficult to see her boss as untrustworthy, despite plenty of evidence that she is?

```

```

- Stephanie's behavior on the morning of the performance evaluation gives some clues about her subsequent conduct at the meeting. What behavior did Stephanie exhibit that morning that Bryony, had she been wiser, could have picked up on and interpreted differently?

```

```

- What does Stephanie fear so much that it results in her acting like this toward her high-performing team member?

```

```

- If Bryony mishandles her subsequent meeting with her boss what does she stand to lose?

```

```

- Having been given a clear ultimatum by her manager, Bryony now has a difficult decision to make. What should her next move be?

LEARNING FROM BRYONY'S MISTAKES

The final section of this chapter provides a summary of the key issues that Bryony mishandles. Each of the bullet points below relates, in order, to one of the questions above. You might like to read each answer and compare it with the notes that you jotted down:

- Up until her performance evaluation meeting Bryony consistently extends trust to Stephanie despite evidence that her manager's conduct isn't worthy of trust. What behavioral evidence does Bryony foolishly ignore?

There is clear behavioral evidence that Stephanie is an unwise person for Bryony to extend trust to. In fact Stephanie fairs poorly on all four criteria for trust presented in the preceding chapter. Firstly, she does not act with integrity. She uses lies and threats to get her own way, and can also be evasive, distorting facts and information if she thinks it will be to her advantage to do so. Secondly, she is unreliable. She is not known for her timely attendance at meetings and regularly turns up late or not at all. She uses her seniority to reschedule meetings at short notice and solely for her convenience, expecting her staff to fall in with the new arrangements no matter what existing commitments they have scheduled. Thirdly, Stephanie is not dependable. She does not exhibit behavior which is, by and large, constant and steady. Instead she is a law unto herself and accountable to no one. Fourthly, having failed to perceive these traits for what they are, it is not surprising that Bryony fails to realize that Stephanie's gesture of goodwill – getting her tickets for the Flushing Meadow Men's Singles Final – is more a useful ploy than a genuine expression of good faith. This act, procuring a pair of highly sought after tickets for Bryony, is misinterpreted by Bryony as a sign of Stephanie's positive regard for their relationship. Actually, it is a useful way for Stephanie to wrong-foot Bryony and put her off guard, creating room for the manipulations that Stephanie ultimately employs when it suits her in the performance evaluation meeting.

■ Bryony also fails to recognize Stephanie's behavior as untrusting and untrustworthy, preferring to interpret it as idiosyncratic rather than duplicitous. What behavioral evidence does she overlook in assessing her manager's character?

There is clear behavioral evidence of Stephanie's preference for using untrusting behavior on three of the four objective criteria. As we will see, the fourth criterion is also open to interpretation. Firstly, Stephanie does not use open behavior with anyone, even with those she has lunch with and goes for a drink with, like Bryony. This is quite deliberate, and means that Stephanie can keep her ear to the ground and her cards close to her chest when talking with her colleagues. It also means she can ask questions, find out useful information and listen while giving nothing away. She stores away whatever useful tit bits she picks up for use later on, as and when the need arises. Secondly, Stephanie never takes risks, and doesn't give information or convey anything useful to anyone else unless she has to. Her approach to communicating with her colleagues is characterized by her giving nothing but expecting everything. She doesn't give to get, she expects to get without giving. Thirdly, Stephanie doesn't share anything with Bryony that she doesn't have to. Sure, if she needs to give her information to enable her to do her job, she will. But she purposefully withholds all other information to retain power and control, and to make sure that the distance she needs to maintain between her and her colleague is firmly preserved. Lastly, while Stephanie does not monitor Bryony's actions that closely, sadly, Bryony misinterprets this lack of monitoring as a sign that her manager is using trusting behavior with her. In fact Stephanie's failure to monitor her team member is simply because she knows she doesn't have to. Stephanie learns early on that her top performing team member is a self-starter, proactive and competent. This combination of qualities means that Stephanie can safely leave Bryony to her own devices, knowing she will do a good job and will keep her updated about progress. This approach means that Stephanie can leave Bryony to get on with it, and can use the time she would otherwise have had to spend managing her report in other ways. However, should Bryony ever mess up, Stephanie would be all over her like a rash and would not hold back voicing her feelings, no matter how many flawless months work Bryony put in preceding her error. If Bryony was a more astute judge of character she would realize that the absence of monitoring displayed by her manager is not evidence of goodwill at all, it is simply evidence of an absence of monitoring.

■ Why do you think Bryony finds it so difficult to see her boss as untrustworthy despite plenty of evidence that she is?

Bryony is basically a nonpolitical and trusting person. Crucially, she wants to believe that her boss is ok too. Being fundamentally good, she blinds herself to her manager's true motives and prefers to see her as someone who is different from her, but not reprehensible. She needs to believe in her boss because she works with her and for her, and because she wants to avoid the conflict that she would experience if she, an honest person, realized that she was working closely with someone disreputable and dishonest.

■ Stephanie's behavior on the morning of the performance evaluation gives some clues about her subsequent conduct at the meeting. What behavior did Stephanie exhibit that morning that Bryony, had she been wiser, could have picked up on and interpreted differently?

Stephanie has a reputation for being late for some meetings and not turning up at all for others. However, even for her, her behavior on the morning of the performance evaluation has all the hallmarks of a deliberate maneuver and needs to be handled as such by Bryony. Bryony would have helped herself by being on the lookout for discrepancies between what Stephanie said she would do and what she actually does do. And each time such a situation arose she needed to confront it, professionally but firmly. This strategy would not have prevented Stephanie from adopting the course of action she did, but it would have preserved Bryony's power more effectively than she managed to do by getting angry and feeling frustrated. Firstly, Bryony ought to have noticed that her manager wasn't in on time and taken it as a signal that something was up. Stephanie might have been sick, or handling an emergency, so Bryony's first reaction should have been to keep cool and get some facts. Having got those facts – that Stephanie had rung in to say she would be late – Bryony should have picked up on the fact that the message Stephanie left did not specifically reassure Bryony that Stephanie would make the 0930 meeting. This omission ought to have been seen by Bryony as a red flag, a small one, but a red one nonetheless. Secondly, after Stephanie arrives at work, she asks her PA to send an e-mail to Bryony rescheduling the meeting for 1330. Another red flag. The e-mail makes no apology for Stephanie missing the first meeting and doesn't offer any explanation for the rearrangement. At this point Bryony could have gone straight to Stephanie's desk and let her know that she would be expecting the meeting to go ahead at 1330. If Stephanie then postponed it again – which does, of course, happen – Bryony could have canceled it herself, saying that she'd rather the meeting be rescheduled to a date and time when her boss had the mental space to attend to it fully. This strategy would have been respectful to Stephanie, would have reframed the issues as Bryony wanting to help her boss on a particularly busy day, would have given Stephanie the signal that Bryony isn't going to fobbed off, and could have prevented the power play that ensued when the meeting took place at 1500. By allowing Stephanie to repeatedly reschedule the meeting, Bryony let her manager control the situation and manipulate her. She lost her way, ended up on the back foot and was completely unprepared for the confusing and unexpected meeting that ensued.

- What does Stephanie fear so much that it results in her acting like this toward her high-performing team member?

Stephanie fears that her top performing team member is a potential fly in her ointment. She fears that Bryony might be promoted over her head, might become more influential in the department than she is, or might get the ear of the senior managers who don't like the way Stephanie operates. Stephanie knows she has enemies in the organization – anyone who sails as close to the wind as she does will make enemies – and she doesn't want Bryony getting too close to them. She also fears that if Bryony continues to do as well as she has been doing, then someone from outside the department will offer her a bigger and better role, and Stephanie will lose a team member with a mammoth appetite for work. Stephanie is lazy and can't afford to let this happen. Also, deep down Stephanie is uncomfortable, even threatened, by her team member's goodness. Stephanie gets things done by manipulating and coercing people. Bryony gets things done by working hard and building rapport with people. Stephanie is basically dishonest, Bryony is basically honest. Stephanie fears that Bryony's values around integrity and openness will destabilize her power base in her own department if she allows Bryony to continue to gain in reputation and influence. She fears that, somehow, Bryony may, even if she doesn't intend to, expose the dubious side of Stephanie's workplace conduct. Stephanie sees Bryony as a threat and she, Stephanie, has a lot to lose. She is threatened by Bryony's goodness *and* success, a potent combination for someone who is neither good nor successful in her own right, and whose progress in the group has been, to some extent, through manipulating the system, taking credit for other people's work and managing the perceptions of those above her whose opinion matters.

- If Bryony mishandles her subsequent meeting with her boss what does she stand to lose?

If Bryony mishandles the fallout from the performance evaluation meeting she has a lot to lose. Stephanie wants to scare her; to confuse and disorient her, to make her uncertain so she can use her confusion to ascertain if she can, really, be brought into Stephanie's shady fold. The performance evaluation meeting is the vehicle Stephanie chooses for this maneuver, because Stephanie knows that Bryony will attend it in buoyant mood, off guard and expecting a top rating. If Stephanie can wrong-foot Bryony enough to get her into her power, she will neutralize her and stop her from potentially exposing Stephanie and her methods in the future. If Bryony mishandles the subsequent meeting she could lose at least some of her integrity, her self-esteem, her confidence and her self-respect. As far as her career goes she could get an unjustly poor performance evaluation rating and an unjustly poor bonus payment. She may not get future promotions her work merits as long as Stephanie remains her manager.

- Having been given a clear ultimatum by her manager, Bryony now has a difficult decision to make. What should her next move be?

Stephanie leaves the performance evaluation meeting giving Bryony a choice, receive a poor performance evaluation rating now or come back having thought about it and maybe get a better rating if she says enough of the right things. Bryony needs to act carefully but decisively. She needs to determine what matters more to her: her integrity or her performance evaluation rating. She needs to make it clear to her boss – preferably within the hour – that her integrity isn't up for grabs. She needs to stick to her guns that her performance speaks for itself, is documented and factual, and that she expects to be appraised on the basis of her performance and nothing else. She may even want to say that the values differences between her and Stephanie are not relevant to the performance evaluation, and that she would expect Stephanie to leave them at the door. If Stephanie reacts angrily or explosively, Bryony needs to firmly but clearly repeat all of this again and, if necessary, a third or fourth time until she is heard. Whatever happens after the performance evaluation meeting Stephanie's conduct at it has changed her relationship with Bryony forever. Bryony's relationship with her manager will not recover and will, from that moment onwards, be very difficult to manage. But acting wisely, and in this way, will protect Bryony from coercion and might just protect her from an unjust outcome from her performance evaluation meeting. She will also learn a lot about how to interpret her manager's behavior in the future, and about how much her own self-deceptions about her manager's true motives ultimately hurt her by blinding her to the truth about Stephanie's ill intent.

This case study has focused on how an inaccurate set of judgments about a manager's trustworthiness and political motives can backfire on a hardworking but naïve young manager. It has illustrated the fact that it is far better to face the ugly truth about a colleague's motives and untrustworthiness, and deal with that reality wisely, than it is to attribute more benign or neutral motives to colleagues whose behavior doesn't warrant that interpretation. The case study demonstrates the value of using the four criteria presented in the preceding chapter to help make an accurate assessment about whether or not to trust a colleague; and the value of using the four objective criteria for assessing trusting or untrusting behavior to help round out the picture.

The following chapter will change tack. It will propose responses you could make when faced with each of 14 key political behaviors at work, responses which will enable you to handle each of the behaviors effectively and convincingly.

Responding to Key Political Behaviors

In previous chapters we have examined a wide variety of issues surrounding political behavior at work. We have defined political behavior as behavior that is designed to help a person achieve their own internally driven agenda, rather than the goals of their role. We've seen how the richness of different value systems and the different styles people use at work add levels of complexity to workplace political dynamics. We've also examined, in some depth, how to go about working effectively with politically minded people in order to get things done, how to assess the political roles that you and your colleagues adopt on certain issues, how to judge the level of trust that exists in your working relationships and how to make the most of the personal power and organizational influence available to you in your role.

It's time now to look in specific detail at a further range of political behaviors that you might find in your own workplace, ones which we haven't yet touched on in previous chapters of the book. The aim of this chapter is to outline a series of 14 additional political behaviors that are commonly used in organizations so that you can:

- Identify which of these behaviors you have observed being used in your workplace.
- Review a set of tactics that you could use as a starting point for handling each of the political behaviors should you be confronted with any of them at work.
- Determine which of the political behaviors you use in the workplace – and assess what impact using these behaviors has on your work and working relationships.

THE BREADTH OF POLITICAL BEHAVIORS AT WORK

There are many, many behaviors which you will encounter at work which, given the definition of political behavior introduced in Chapter 2, constitute political activity. Some of them may well not have a particularly unhelpful or unproductive impact on their initiator's reputation or the quality of their relationships with their colleagues. Others, however, may turn out to be both divisive and destructive to the initiator, to their relationships with their colleagues and to their organization's ability to reach its goals.

One of the main reasons nonpolitically minded people struggle to handle politically motivated behavior in their colleagues is that they don't, at the time it is being used, recognize the behavior for what it is. They are either blind to the true motivation behind the actions they observe and consequently mishandle them; or, lacking information about what constitutes political behavior in the first place, incorrectly ascribe a nonpolitical motive to political actions and respond ineffectively to them. This chapter will equip you with the information you need to accurately identify an additional 14 commonly used workplace political behaviors. It will also outline an effective strategy that you could use to handle each of the behaviors should you need to.

HANDLING 14 KEY POLITICAL BEHAVIORS

The 14 political tactics presented in this chapter are not intended to be an exhaustive catalog of the political behaviors not touched on elsewhere in the book. As you read through the description of each of the political behaviors, I'd like you to recall a specific example of where you witnessed the behavior being used at work – or where you were on the receiving end of it. Don't worry if you cannot recall an exact replica of each of the situations described down to the fine details. Focus instead on recalling instances which mirror the dynamics being described. You can use the space below each example to write down your feelings and observations about the instances you recall.

Following each space for your notes you will find a description of an effective tactic for handling the political dynamic that has just been described. These descriptions are entitled 'handling the politics'. They focus on steps you could take to respond effectively to each of the 14 key political behaviors so that, should you find yourself confronted by any these tactics, you know what to do in response.

Often the response I suggest involves, at least to some extent, that you 'name the game'. Verbally labeling a political behavior by its name, and therefore telling the user of the behavior that you recognize the motive behind the behavior, unmasks the political strategy for the game that it is, and forces the user of the behavior to change tack. Being confronted in this way is embarrassing, even if the dialog is only between you and the other person, and there are no other witnesses. It causes the other person to cease using the political strategy, and replace it with a more productive behavior instead. However, remember that from their reaction at the time you might not know that your words have had any effect. A truly political operator won't show you what they feel, so don't worry if you can't see any obvious signs of embarrassment. The behavior will cease from then on, at least with you. When you 'name the game' you need to use a normal conversational tone for maximum effect.

THREE CATEGORIES OF POLITICAL BEHAVIOR

The 14 political behaviors outlined below are divided into three categories. In each case the category title refers to the behavior which the initiator of the political tactic uses. The three category titles are as follows:

- Avoiding responsibility: These are political behaviors that enable your colleague to avoid responsibility for their actions and, when things have gone wrong, to shift responsibility – and therefore culpability – elsewhere.
- Controlling behaviors: These are political behaviors designed to retain your colleague's power and control over decisions and courses of action, and are usually used in the context of a meeting.
- Individual motivations: These are political behaviors which are driven by your colleague's specific inner agenda.

Let's start by considering five behaviors which fall under the category of avoiding responsibility.

Avoiding Responsibility

1 Creating a Scapegoat

One of your colleagues has messed up on an important project, and decides to cover her back by placing the blame elsewhere. She tells everyone who will listen to her – both face-to-face and on e-mail – that what has gone wrong isn't her fault at all but is somebody else's, someone who she names. This person is, in fact, not blameworthy at all, although they are a plausible scapegoat because they have been involved in the project.

- The political dynamic: Afraid at the potential consequences of her mistake, and wanting to deflect attention from it quickly and effectively, your colleague creates a scapegoat. She does this by blaming an innocent bystander, hoping that others will be fooled by the ploy and attack the other person instead of her. She does this to avoid having to take personal responsibility for messing up, and/or because she is afraid that she will be publically blamed – and humiliated – by her manager for what has gone wrong. By creating a scapegoat early on in this way she hopes to deflect attention away from her own culpability and put it on to someone else in the hope that they will end up carrying the can for her instead.

- Handling the politics: Your colleague could send an e-mail to everyone involved in project, and to everyone who has received the e-mail about her. It should set out, calmly and clearly, all the facts of the matter. It could say that it is true she was involved in the project, but that her role was as number two, meaning that she did not have primary responsibility for it. She could point out that she did not take any of the key decisions, and that, consequently, she is concerned to note that her senior project colleague appears to be attempting to shift blame onto *her* for the recent errors and mistakes. She could end by saying that she would like to refocus the debate around the true issues which are that her colleague has made a number of recent errors that will need to be addressed. She should copy the e-mail to the person who tried to scapegoat her. If you are on the receiving end of the tactic of creating a scapegoat the important thing is to react factually. Don't attack the person who has created the scapegoat, don't point out their failings and flaws, but keep calm and respond with clear facts. Facts are very powerful at confronting the tactic of scapegoating and, in the end, the truth speaks for itself.

2 Reducing People to Numbers

One of your senior managers has to make a difficult decision, such as deciding who will be made redundant, or whose job will be relocated far away, or whose role will be significantly changed against their wishes. He handles the stress inherent in making these life-changing decisions about other people by thinking about, and starting to treat the people involved, as data or numbers. This tactic makes the decision more manageable for him but leaves the people treated this way feeling simply awful.

■ The political dynamic: Reducing people to numbers enables difficult decisions to seem more manageable in the minds of those charged with making them. But it actually results in human beings being treated as objects. They feel that they are being reduced to statistics and data, and the strategy causes a lot of distress and upset.

■ Handling the politics: If you are on the receiving end of this tactic, you need to confront the fact that your self-esteem has been injured. You might want to leave your response until after the decisions have been announced. Your aim is not to influence the decisions or, if they are unfavorable to you, overturn them. Instead it is to tell your manager what you think about the style with which he has made those decisions. You might start by saying that you wouldn't wish to be in his shoes, and that you recognize that the decisions he has been charged with making over recent weeks have been very challenging. You might go on to say that nonetheless you consider the way in which he has made those decisions has been poor, that by reducing people to objects he has hurt them and been, to say the least, disrespectful and inconsiderate. You could say that by reducing people to numbers he may have made his job easier, but he has compounded the difficulty of losing their jobs for everyone involved. You could end by telling him that you are not saying this out of chagrin at the decision. Nor are you trying to get him to change his mind. You are telling him this because you want him to hear the feedback. Having said this, don't wait for a reaction, just leave the meeting and let him think about it.

3 Automatic Cynicism

One of your colleagues dismisses every new idea that either you or anyone else originates instantly and completely. She either labels the new idea as 'pointless' or 'a waste of time'. The impulse to do this is her strong inner cynicism, not a reasoned, well thought-out objection to the proposals, and she can be counted on to utter her pronouncements with some emotion.

- The political dynamic: Your colleague automatically reacts to any new or stimulating idea with cynicism, a reaction which is energy sapping and annoying for everyone else to have to deal with. She does this to avoid having to consider anything new and to avoid having to adopt new ways of working. She can therefore avoid the responsibility of having to change, learn, develop or adapt, and can continue to do things in the current way that is comfortable for her, even if it is ineffective and inefficient. She effectively withdraws her co-operation from those initiating change and hopes to get away with it. This is a passive form of aggression aimed at undermining them and what they are doing.

- Handling the politics: Someone needs to confront the fact that this colleague reacts with automatic cynicism at every opportunity. A quizzical comment such as 'more cynicism?' would be a good place to start. Whatever her reply, a further comment such as 'why do you dismiss every new idea without thinking about it?' would hold her accountable for her actions, and make it very difficult for her to be as verbally cynical next time. She may still have cynical thoughts, but at least the people within earshot won't have to hear them.

4 Stalling

You are waiting for one of your IT colleagues to complete the background research on the cost benefits of upgrading your team's office network. She had promised that she'd have a decision about whether or not to proceed two weeks ago. When approached about the delay she claims to be busily working away examining the options, and makes positive noises about the different possibilities she is exploring, highlighting the advantages that the new system would have over the current one. You think she is dragging her feet over making the decision and actually doing nothing about it while appearing publicly supportive of it, at least in principle.

■ The political dynamic: Your IT colleague has a hard time saying 'no'. As an alternative to saying 'no' she outwardly complies and then does nothing behind the scenes. Too embarrassed to admit her original mistake, she compounds the problem when challenged and lies, saying that she is working on it when she isn't. While this isn't the smartest tactic, and eventually it will become clear, if you push hard enough, that nothing has happened, it does buy her time and means that she doesn't have to do something she finds hard to do. This is say 'no' and risk disappointing you.

■ Handling the politics: You need to ask a series of specific questions which will force her to come clean. You could start by asking her where she has got to with the project. Then you could ask her what the delay is about, who else is involved in the research, what the deadline is and in what way she will communicate her decision to you. These questions are designed to put her on the back foot as they are all perfectly reasonable questions but ones to which she has no answer. You could then ask her what criteria she has developed to help her reach the decision and what right of appeal you have should you not like the decision. Finally, you could say something like, 'you're not really doing anything about this are you?' If you are not comfortable with the reply you could suggest that you arrange a meeting between the two of you, and your two bosses, to measure progress. This tack ought to force her to come clean. If she doesn't own up then you can at least arrange this meeting and, hopefully, either make some real progress or come to the conclusion that the project isn't going anywhere and address that point.

5 Justifying

You have asked your colleague from facilities management to review the options for rehousing your team in a larger office in the same building. He comes back after two weeks and says it won't be possible to do this as there isn't any available office space large enough to take your expanding team. Three days later, you discover that there is a good-sized, light room unoccupied on the tenth floor. You call him and ask why he hasn't suggested that you move into that room. Your colleague gives you a series of explanations, some of them convoluted and hard to follow, to clarify why he hasn't put your team forward for a move to the tenth floor. He suggests that the room is damp, inconveniently located on an upper floor, is earmarked for another team – but he cannot remember which – and, because it is several floors up, would require that he hired in extra help which is an expensive undertaking simply for a move. He further suggests that since everyone else is coping with cramped accommodation he is sure your team can too. You are exasperated by the fact that you cannot get a straight answer to a straight question, and the more you try to pin him down the more slippery he becomes. However, you realize he doesn't favor the proposed move and back down.

- The political dynamic: Your colleague is lazy and irresponsible. He is quite comfortable doing the bits of his job that he enjoys while ignoring his duty to carry out the other, more complex and difficult tasks. He doesn't want to have to work hard at a large and challenging office move, especially one which will take place at a weekend, so doesn't do the research, never seriously considers the options for rehousing your team in a new office, and then tries to fob you off. He doesn't answer any of your points clearly, changes the emphasis of the conversation frequently and develops explanations which are designed to throw you off the scent. These explanations make his decision not to recommend your team's move to the tenth floor office space appear credible. They appear to justify it but, actually, their real purpose is to create fog around his laziness and dislike of a key aspect of his role. He hopes you'll fall for it and go away.

- Handling the politics: You need to challenge your colleague on his justifications for why your team cannot move office. But you need to do so in a very specific way. The more you ask sensible questions about the whys and wherefores of the move, the more you look for rational reasons why the move can or cannot go ahead, the more you take what he says at face value, the stronger he will get. Your best strategy involves you assuming he isn't playing it straight with you and is avoiding responsibility. Personalize your ensuing disappointment at this conclusion, rather than arguing the merits of the case with him. This is much more likely to break through this complacency. You might say to him 'I am disappointed that you are telling me that we cannot move to the tenth floor' followed by 'I am not satisfied with what I am hearing. I would like to take this further and explore the possibility in more detail. I will do so and get back to you'. This tells him that his tactics haven't worked. You at the least suspect him of being dilatory and you are prepared to act to verify the situation. By taking this tack you are retaining control and placing yourself in charge of the process from that point onwards. However, you must be prepared to back up your words with action, investigate and get back to him. You might find that in the meantime the room has suddenly become available and he can move your team into it after all.

Let's now move on to examine four behaviors that are commonly used to control the process, content and outcomes of meetings.

Controlling Behaviors

6 Using Silence to Control Meetings

You have been invited to a meeting, along with several other people, and are looking forward to an opportunity to discuss the issues openly and fully. The meeting is being chaired by someone senior to you and you know that he has a vested interest in the outcome of the meeting. However, what you aren't banking on is that, early on in the meeting, he starts to signal his disapproval of the views of some people at the meeting through clear and sustained silence. Other people at the meeting quickly pick up on these powerful cues and fewer attendees participate verbally in the meeting from that point on. Those who do don't say very much.

- The political dynamic: The chair employs the tactic of using silence to control the meeting. His powerful silences effectively control whether or not other participants speak and, if they do speak, what they say. This tactic ensures that those people whose views he doesn't like keep quiet or, if they do speak, they don't get support from anyone else at the meeting. This way he can steer the meeting down the course he wants it to take, and make sure that he gets the outcome he wants from the meeting.

- Handling the politics: This is a tricky one and you need to tread cautiously. The chair has more organizational authority than you, and is using that influence to control the meeting. You need to take a tack which preserves your personal power but which ensures that you don't incur the disfavor of the chair. If you still want to put the points you would have made at the meeting to him, do so in an e-mail after the meeting, saying what you need to say, but doing so in a way that won't get you into public or private trouble. The tone of the e-mail needs to be helpful and you need to position it as a service to the chair. You might say that you have been reflecting on the content of the meeting and would like to draw a few points to his attention. Don't use your e-mail to evaluate his behavior at the meeting, criticize his approach to chairing the meeting or argue with what he did. Respect his position as someone senior to you, and accept that you don't know enough about the pressures on him to understand why he chose to handle things as he did. Make your e-mailed points factually, and let him get on with it.

7 Abruptly Ending A Discussion

You are invited to a meeting which is being chaired by someone with more organizational authority than you. The chair introduces the agenda items one at a time but, from early on, ends discussion on an item, as far as you are concerned, prematurely and before full discussion of it has taken place. She then swiftly moves the debate on to another topic, justifying her action by saying that there is much to get through on the agenda and little time left.

- The political dynamic: The person chairing the meeting employs the tactic of abruptly ending a discussion. She is actually ending the discussion at a point she thinks is advantageous for her. These points often coincide with the introduction by her of her points of view. She is motivated by her concern that her wishes will not be supported at the meeting if discussion ensues. She ends discussions prematurely because this gives her room to maneuver outside the meeting. When discussing the way forward with her peers and senior managers after the meeting, she can say that the meeting ended with broad agreement about her plans, and change the subject.

- Handling the politics: This is also a tricky one and once more you need to tread cautiously. You could handle this situation in a similar way to the previous example, by sending an e-mail to the chair after the meeting making your points in a nonevaluative way. Or, you may decide that there isn't much to be gained in this situation, and you should put your energy to use elsewhere. If it's important to you, you may decide to e-mail her with the views you would have given had the meeting been conducted in a more open manner.

8 Holding a Corridor Meeting

You are invited to attend a meeting by a more senior colleague and accept the invitation. You are told in the invitation that the purpose of the meeting is to make a decision on an issue that affects your current key project at work. You find out that several other interested parties have been invited and are also attending. However, it becomes apparent during the meeting that it is not a decision-making forum at all. The person who has called the meeting isn't really listening to your views, although he should be, nor is he listening to the views of the other people in the meeting. In fact, as the meeting progresses, it becomes clear that the decision has already been made beforehand – in the corridor or in an adjoining room – by a few people only, one of whom is the person who called the meeting and invited you.

- The political dynamic: The chair, and probably one or two of his close allies, have already held a corridor meeting in advance of this meeting at which they have already made their decision. Despite this they still go ahead and organize the meeting which they claim will be a decision-making forum. Their pre-meeting decision is both fixed and firm, which reduces the meeting you attend to a hollow exercise, wasting the time of everyone present. This tactic effectively stops all the other participants in the meeting from having an input to the decision, and retains power in the hands of the few. No matter what is said by you or anyone else, the decision has already been made without wider consultation, and will not now be changed.

- Handling the politics: This is a question of power and you need to decide what action, if any, you want to take. If you think that the quality of the decision is good, then you might not feel the need to do anything further this time round. However, if you think the decision is flawed, you might want to e-mail your objections to the people who attended the meeting, pointing out the possible negative consequences of the decision. Your e-mail should be respectful in tone and factual, highlighting what you think might happen if the decision stands. This approach – highlighting the possible adverse consequences of the decision – will cause the chair and his allies to think twice. It may be too late to undo this decision, but in future, they may well approach you for a view and take your opinions into account.

9 Hearing Silence as Agreement

The person chairing a meeting you are attending makes a contentious proposal. A silence ensues in which you and the other participants consider what she said and weigh up whether or not it is worth making an opposing point. She lets the silence go for a while and then says 'that's agreed then', before moving the meeting on to other topics. No one objects and the meeting moves on.

- The political dynamic: Hearing silence as agreement enables the chair to make sure that her will prevails at the meeting on that issue, and effectively stops all further debate on the issue.

```
┌─────────────────────────────────────────────────────────────┐
│                                                             │
│                                                             │
│                                                             │
│                                                             │
│                                                             │
└─────────────────────────────────────────────────────────────┘
```

- Handling the politics: Once more, you need to decide whether or not you want to take any action following the use of this tactic by the chair. If you do, you could wait until the end of the following agenda item, and then interject, saying that you've had second thoughts about the previous issue and would like to make a few points. In doing this, don't necessarily expect support for your views or the fact of your input. Only do it if you want to make your points and then expect the meeting to move on.

Finally, let's take a look at five behaviors which reflect the individual motivations of the initiator of the political tactic.

Individual Motivations

10 Verbal Withdrawal

You are in a meeting with several other people, and there is a sharp difference of opinion. One of your colleagues realizes that his strongly held point of view is not supported by anyone else. He handles his discomfort at this situation by deciding not to participate verbally in the meeting from that point on. He pushes back from the table, folds his arms and, while remaining present at the table, chooses to remain silent.

- The political dynamic: Annoyed and chagrined at not getting his own way, your colleague decides to withdraw his input from the meeting. His verbal withdrawal results in him remaining physically present at the table, but he sulks to signal his displeasure that his colleagues have not supported his point of view. The meeting loses his input, energy and creativity, simply because his views aren't supported and he isn't going to get his way.

```
┌─────────────────────────────────────────────────────────────┐
│                                                             │
│                                                             │
│                                                             │
│                                                             │
│                                                             │
└─────────────────────────────────────────────────────────────┘
```

- Handling the politics: Someone needs to confront the fact that this colleague has verbally withdrawn from the meeting. This should ideally happen at the meeting, shortly after your colleague has verbally withdrawn from it. Posing a question to him such as 'why have you opted out of the meeting?' would be a good place to start. Whatever his reply, a further comment such as 'it comes over that you have left the meeting' would hold him accountable for his actions, and make it very difficult for him to remain withdrawn. These words contain a hint of regret that he has withdrawn from the meeting. It is highly unlikely that he'd remain emotionally absent from the meeting after being called to account in this way.

11 Acting Behind Your Back

A colleague needs to resolve a conflict with you before you can make progress on the issues holding back your joint project. She wants to take one course of action, but knows that you strongly favor an alternative approach. You expect her to discuss the issues openly and calmly with you, so you can find a constructive way forward together. But, you realize that she has decided to avoid the conflict altogether and isn't going to speak with you to find a jointly agreed solution. In fact, you find out that she has already taken unilateral action behind your back. She hopes that handling things this way will enable her to act independently of you and take the project down her preferred route before you find out and after it's too late for you to do anything purposeful about it.

- The political dynamic: In order to sidestep having to resolve a conflict, and to facilitate her getting her own way, your colleague takes matters into her own hands. She hopes the confusion she creates will enable her to take the unilateral action she favors, and which she knows you don't favor, and that it'll be too late for you to undo her actions once you find out.

■ Handling the politics: As soon as you find out what has happened you need to go to your colleague and confront her. It is likely to be too late to undo the course of events she has set in train behind your back, but you can make sure that she thinks twice before using this tactic with you again. You might want to make it clear to her that you are disappointed at the way she has acted, and that you are holding her accountable for her conduct. You might say something like, 'I am disappointed that you avoided speaking with me about the issues between us and then took unilateral action behind my back. I don't want you to handle things in this way again'. While you cannot stop her from doing something similar in the future, your strongest suite is to suggest to her, with some feeling, that, if she acts in a similar fashion in the future, you will have something to say about it. This will put a doubt into her mind, and make her think about the possible ways in which you might react should she do the same sort of thing again. It also makes it clear that you are choosing not to act this time, but, equally, will choose to act if she does this again. This is an important point to get across, because it makes it clear to her that she hasn't managed to control you or your actions, either this time or on a subsequent occasion. Quite the opposite. It is you who is in charge of what you do and how you react, and while you are taking a lenient line this time, you won't if it happens again. This approach will force your colleague to consider the consequences for her if she uses this tactic again. However, should she put you to the test and repeat her political tactic, you'd have to be prepared to act and make waves for her, otherwise she will instantly learn that you don't back up your words with action, and you will have shot yourself in the foot.

12 Saying One Thing, Doing Another

Your colleague makes an agreement with you over a key contentious issue, an agreement to which, at the time of making it, he has no real commitment. You, of course, don't realize this at the time and think he is being sincere in his wish to work constructively with you. He makes the agreement – saying one thing – in order to make it look as if he is working collaboratively with you, when actually he doesn't want to collaborate with you at all. At some point down the road, he goes against his word and does a different thing entirely, so that, without your knowledge, he can go and do whatever he wants to do anyway. He hopes that you will not find out that he has done this until it's too late for you to do anything purposeful about it.

- The political dynamic: In order to avoid the time, effort and inter-personal investment needed to build a constructive working relationship with you, your colleague says one thing and does another instead. It's too time consuming for him to really work through the outstanding issues with you, and he wants to be able to act independently of you as and when he chooses. So he creates room for maneuver by letting you form the impression that he is working with you. He does this to throw you off guard so that, at some point down the road when your attention is elsewhere, he can break the 'agreement' he has made with you and do something else, unilaterally, instead.

- Handling the politics: As soon as you find out what has happened you need to confront your colleague. You might want to go to him and point out the discrepancy between what you were expecting to happen and what has actually happened, before asking him to account for how this state of affairs has come to exist. This opening will put your colleague right on the spot and force him to explain his actions. It will be much more effective than complaining about what he has done, getting angry or threatening to escalate the issues.

13 Scoring Points Off Colleagues

Your colleague has recently done a poor job on an important piece of work. In the subsequent weeks, she makes a number of unpleasant remarks about your work, work which is actually going well. She denigrates your efforts, trying to suggest that your approach is flawed and highlights specific aspects of your performance which she thinks are below par.

- The political dynamic: Your colleague is using the tactic of scoring points off you. She does this to divert attention from her own failure, and in the hope that she can undermine you and cause you to doubt yourself, just as she now doubts herself. Instead of confronting her own poor performance and learning how to handle her work more effectively in future, she tries to reduce your enjoyment of your work by making pointed and, she hopes, demoralizing comments about your work in your hearing.

■ Handling the politics: The next time your colleague makes a point scoring comment you need to confront her. You could say, 'another attempt to score points off me?' or 'another attempt to undermine me?' She won't try this behavior with you again, although she might move on to someone else instead.

14 *Taking Credit for Other People's Work*

You have been working with a colleague on a joint project for your senior managers on the management team. You, in particular, are also snowed under. Unfortunately, the meeting at which you are to present your work to the management team coincides with another meeting you need to attend. Your colleague kindly suggests that he go to the management team meeting alone and present on behalf of you both. You are not sure this is a good idea, and so say. But your colleague says that it'd be the best way forward for you and would save you some time. You agree. You subsequently regret your decision when you realize that he has downplayed your role in the work, and played up his own role, presenting himself to the senior management team as the person mainly responsible for work which was actually a joint endeavor.

■ The political dynamic: Your colleague takes advantage of your heavy workload for his own ends. He engineers a situation where he can misrepresent your input, take credit for your work and promote himself in the eyes of his senior managers. He is particularly divisive in his methods, as he actually suggests to you that it would be in your best interests not to attend the meeting and to let him take the strain for you. What he really has in mind is to get you out of the way so he can take all the available kudos and praise, while making sure that you don't get as much credit as you should do for your work.

- Handling the politics: You need to confront your colleague *and* set the record straight with your senior management team. The managers first: you could send them all an e-mail, copied to your colleague, in which you set out in cool, factual terms what has happened. You might start by saying that you recognize that your colleague has presented the outcomes of your joint work to them, and that while doing so you understand that it might have come across that the work was mainly the product of his efforts; that actually you worked together throughout the project; and that you consider the two of you to be equally responsible for the outputs. You might also like to say that your colleague had suggested to you that he could attend the meeting himself as a courtesy to you out of respect for your heavy workload. This e-mail doesn't attack your colleague, but presents facts which enable the management team to make up their own mind about what has happened. Then you need to confront your colleague. Tell him that his actions have adversely affected your relationship with him, that you have fully comprehended them. Whatever response you get back, repeat what you have said and leave the meeting. Your tone needs to be calm, adult and considered throughout, not emotional or angry.

WHY PEOPLE USE THESE BEHAVIORS

These 14 behaviors each achieve a specific objective for the person using it. They variously:

- Stop discussion.
- Prevent dissent.
- Require compliance.
- Punish opposition.
- Avoid responsibility.
- Place responsibility elsewhere.
- Remove choice from other people.

Look back at what you wrote below each cameo. Rereading your comments, it might seem that the cost of using these tactics is actually quite high, and that the initiators of these behaviors run the risk of creating a significantly adverse reputation for themselves. You might well have unpleasant memories, even angry ones, when you recall some of the specific instances you wrote about. The habitual users of political behavior such as those instanced above probably don't care that much whether or not they are liked, respected and/or trusted by you or anyone else. What they do value is getting their own way; having power, being in control and avoiding responsibility, so using these 14 tactics – and others like them – makes it more likely that they will get what they want, especially if they are dealing with people unskilled at responding to these behaviors effectively.

YOUR POLITICAL BEHAVIOR

This chapter has focused on providing you with effective tactics for responding to 14 commonly used political behaviors at work. You might now like to consider the 14 behaviors outlined above in relation to yourself and answer the following questions. You can jot down your reactions to each question in the space below it:

■ Which of the 14 political behaviors outlined above have you used in, say, the past month?

■ Think back to a specific instance in which you used at least one of the political behaviors outlined above. What impact did your use of this behavior(s) have on the situation at the time?

■ What impact did your use of this behavior(s) have on your relationships with the other people involved in the situation?

■ If you were in that same position again, facing the same issues again, what would you do differently?

SUMMARY AND NEXT CHAPTER

This chapter has focused on:

■ Helping you to recognize the dynamics behind 14 key political behaviors you are likely encounter at work.
■ How you reacted should you have observed these behaviors being used at work.
■ Identifying a set of interpersonal tactics for use when handling each of the 14 behaviors – tactics designed to retain your power, self-esteem and dignity. Many of the tactics involve you in 'naming the game' and/or using the facts of the matter to alter the dynamic that the political behavior has set in play.
■ Examining briefly why people might use these political behaviors at work.
■ Encouraging you to consider specific instances when you might have used some of these behaviors yourself – and on identifying the consequences of doing so for you, your relationships with your colleagues and the work situation you wanted to address.

The next chapter introduces the final of the six main case studies in the book. Building on the themes of this chapter, the last case study illustrates how internal customers and internal suppliers both seek to blame each other for a poor set of results in the business unit. In a difficult encounter the business unit managers, in particular, employ a variety of political behaviors to avoid responsibility for their unit's underperformance, scapegoat the technology team instead and deflect attention away from their own shortcomings.

Poor Service

BACKGROUND AND CHARACTERS

This case study is set in Singapore in an international shipping company's Asia Head Office. The company offers tracked shipping services by air, road, train and sea, and prides itself on being able to tell its customers, day or night, where their shipment is and when it is due to arrive at its destination. The company's technology team has designed leading edge tracking equipment for use on all its parcels, packages and consignments. The technology team head is Lan Xhiao. Her number two is Satoshi. They have worked together for 18 months, since Satoshi moved from the Tokyo office. However, while the tracking technology is effective and well regarded by customers and business units, other aspects of the technology team's performance are not getting such rave reviews.

Over the past six months there have been a growing number of complaints from the business units about the technology team. There have been complaints about the slow speed of response to escalated queries; difficulties in getting hold of technology team members; long delays in getting answers to enquiries about upgrades; several weeks – and sometimes several months – lead-in times for new equipment; and orders for telephone and other start-up kit being misplaced and not subsequently attended to. Business unit heads also complain that their team members have started to call the technology team the Black Hole as requests and complaints go into the Black Hole but not much comes out again. Recently Grant, who heads up the Customer Services business unit, contacted both Lan Xhiao and Satoshi after one of his team leaders Margarite threw up her hands in disgust at what she saw as another technology team delivery failure, and requested that Grant accompany her to a meeting with the technology team managers to sort it out.

Lan Xhiao is actually very protective of her staff, but they could be forgiven for not realizing it. She thinks they have a difficult job to do and that they don't get as much praise – or remuneration – as their skills deserve. She accepts that her team might not be the most assertive or people-orientated group of employees in the company, but she doesn't accept that they are as ineffective or irresponsible as some business units claim. However, her team rarely see her, despite the long hours she works. She delegates the day-to-day running of her team to Satoshi who has superior technology skills to her. She spends a lot of time reporting upwards, working with the head of the business units to define future IT requirements, and with the Board over future company strategy and the role of IT in that strategy. Lan Xhiao is conscientious, overworked, a poor listener and fed up at what she sees as a culture of complaints in the company. She has no time at all for any business unit, as she sees it, scapegoating her group for its own failings. Twice in the past six months she has requested additional budget so that she can offer her staff customer skills training. Twice her request has fallen on deaf ears. Since the installation of the tracking system Lan Xhiao has also made repeated requests for additional headcount and has always been turned down.

Satoshi is a highly skilled technologist who doesn't like conflict and who will, when under pressure, use manipulative and indirect behavior to protect himself and his team. He runs the technology team day-to-day and sees first hand just how overworked his team members are. He has formed the view that while the 24-hour tracking service which his team developed is bringing in more and more business for the company, technologists' salaries have not increased proportionately in return, but complaints have, rudeness from business unit staff has and so has aggression from business unit bosses who want an instant response to an unimportant problem simply because they've decided it should be top priority for the technology team to attend to. Satoshi wants to offer a top class service to all his internal customers, but believes he and his team can only do so much given the amount of work they need to do to maintain the 24-hour tracking service.

Grant is an aggressive, somewhat arrogant and forceful character who is competitive, driven and ambitious. He is poor with detail and is a moderately effective manager who makes up for his lack of managerial skills by working long hours and getting through a prodigious amount of work himself. He doesn't understand the technical side of IT at all, but does recognize that, without technology, his business unit would simply cease to function. He is uncomfortable being in a position where he doesn't have the knowledge he needs to understand the technology his unit relies on. Consequently he is suspicious of the technology team and quick to blame them should anything apparently technology related go wrong. He maintains a fixed view of the technology team as incompetent and unresponsive and enjoys putting the boot in when he can, believing that this approach will keep them on their toes.

Margarite manages the Customer Services business unit on a day-to-day basis. She knows that her team are underperforming and that the figures demonstrate this clearly enough. It's all very well having state-of-the-art tracking facilities, with the consequent increase in business this has created for the company. But her team now needs to cover 24-hour shifts, and needs to deal with hundreds of more customer queries per day with only a ten percent rise in staff numbers in the unit. Margarite knows that, despite all these constraints, she has singularly failed to get on top of the slipping standards in the unit. She has systematically hidden her inability to manage performance standards upwards from her boss, and has instead, repeatedly told him about the technology team's failure to respond to her staff's requests and urgent escalations. This is true, but so is the fact that her failings as a manager have contributed to the poor standards of customer service being provided by the unit. Knowing that Grant is predisposed to blame technology whenever he can makes it very easy for Margarite to create the impression that the real cause of the unit's underperformance is technology's failure to support them effectively.

ARRANGING THE MEETING

Margarite calls Satoshi and arranges a meeting between herself, Satoshi and Lan Xhiao at which to explore the issues between the technology team and her business unit. The meeting is arranged for 3 pm in two days' time. She does not mention that Grant will be attending. She arranges an ambush, hoping that Grant will use the meeting to assert the view that the business unit is slipping behind expected service standards because of the shortcomings in the technology team. Margarite wants Grant to lay down the law, and make it crystal clear that the technology team needs to become more responsive to the business unit and quickly. She hopes that he will take control of proceedings from the start, and scapegoat the technology team so effectively that she can avoid having to account for her poor management of her unit.

On being invited to the meeting Satoshi's initial reaction is positive. He sees it as an opportunity for him and his manager to meet Margarite from the business unit and explore options for improving service provision. His natural dislike of conflict, his consequent failure to anticipate it, and the fact that he doesn't know Grant will be attending means that he hasn't picked up on just how confrontational a meeting Margarite has in mind. Satoshi manages Lan Xhiao's perception of the meeting by telling her some of the story but not all of it. Lan Xhiao knows that there have been an increased number of complaints recently. She also knows that her staff are not always well treated by the business units. However, she does not know the extent of the problem in either case, and Satoshi doesn't bring her up to speed. He merely tells her it is a meeting to discuss on going service provision to the Customer Service business unit.

WHAT HAPPENS AT THE MEETING

Lan Xhiao and Satoshi arrive on time at the meeting room to find that Margarite and Grant are there, exuding impatience and irritation at being kept waiting. It's a bad start and one which sets the tone for the opening remarks which follow. Satoshi comments that he wasn't expecting to see Grant and looks uncomfortable. He realizes that he has misjudged this completely. Lan Xhiao – who is expecting an exploratory meeting – starts by asking for clarification of the purpose behind the discussion. This is the perfect opening for Margarite who outlines a catalog of technology team failures and poor service, most of which Lan Xhiao is unaware about. Lan Xhiao is shocked and turns to Satoshi asking if these observations are true. He is stuck for an answer and comments that 'it's a matter of perception'. Grant picks up on this and goes for it. He says that the business unit deals with the company's paying customers, the technology team are an overhead on their cost centre, he is currently paying for their people to drift about all day being ineffectual, so what are they going to do about it? He is arrogant, pre-emptory, dismissive and rude.

Satoshi finds his voice and, for the second and last time in the meeting, speaks. He cites reason after reason why service is below-par, all of which are down to the business unit's failure to co-operate with his team members. He says that the business unit are poor at providing regular downtime for maintenance to be carried out on their kit. Consequently there is a backlog of essential maintenance issues that need to be addressed and known repairs that need to be attended to. He says that business unit people call out technology team specialists for minor things they could solve themselves – 'they're like babies who need their hand held' – don't listen to the answers they are given, and are rude and abusive to his people on a regular basis. He says that the business unit won't provide his people with space on their floor and they have to come from the adjoining building which takes time. He says that since the installation of the 24-hour tracking system his team is handling twice the number of escalations that a team its size should be dealing with, while also maintaining the tracking system 24/7.

Grant is not prepared to listen to what he considers to be blame shifting. He threatens to contact Lan Xhiao's manager in Hong Kong.

Lan Xhiao leaps in to stop this line of discussion, saying that it won't be necessary and that she'll work with him to resolve whatever difficulties they are having. Margarite then counters with 'Well, what are you going to do then?' effectively putting the ball into Lan Xhiao's court. Lan Xhiao, completely on the back foot, assures her business unit colleagues that things will change for the better. Grant and Margarite, however, won't have any of it and the heat rises in the meeting. To them this is the usual technology team response – things will get better, just give us time – which they have heard before and don't believe. They reiterate that there are fundamental service issues at stake and they need to see actual improvements.

Lan Xhiao turns helplessly to Satoshi, concerned that he has apparently set her up for this fall. She has never mistrusted him before, but, now, for the first time, she is worried that her team is doing much more badly than she realized. She explains her constraints in terms of budget for training and headcount restrictions but Grant and Margarite are not interested. Lan Xhiao feels out of her depth in terms of the service issues the business unit are raising, the interpersonal dynamics at the meeting and her own relationship with Satoshi. She has no facts to work with and has to assume that, until it is proved otherwise, her business unit colleagues are telling the truth. She tries to keep the conversation going, but it degenerates into conflict and counterconflict. The meeting ends with Satoshi opting to leave the fight and with Lan Xhiao apologizing again to Grant and Margarite. She promises to get back to them at the end of the day.

ANALYZING THE POLITICAL DYNAMICS: YOUR ROLE

Consider the following questions. They are designed to help you look behind the facts of the case study and examine the political dynamics at play between Lan Xhiao, Satoshi, Grant and Margarite. You can jot down your answers to each question in the space below it. The first set of questions invite you to analyze the political dynamics involving Lan Xhiao and Satoshi:

■ Satoshi operates out of two hidden agendas in his relationship with his manager. What are they?

- Satoshi tells the business unit that their staff have failed to co-operate with his team. While this is true, he could have made much better use of this fact had he handled it differently. What should he have done instead?

- Lan Xhiao is completely taken aback by the business unit's appraisal of her team's performance. Without any facts to go on, and without any support from the largely silent Satoshi, she is wrong-footed. What mistakes does she make in the meeting?

The second set of questions invites you to analyze the political dynamics involving Grant and Margarite:

- Where the technology team is concerned, Grant operates out of several hidden agendas. What are they?

- Margarite operates out of a hidden agenda in her relationship with her manager. What is it?

- At the meeting Margarite is effective at setting her manager up to scapegoat the technology team for its supposed failure to deliver. What issues does this approach raise for her in the future?

The third set of questions invites you to analyze the political dynamics between the business unit and the technology team:

- Neither the technology team nor the business unit is wholly to blame for their deteriorating relationship, but both are responsible for the lack of co-operation between them. What should each group now do to put things on an even keel?

- Satoshi and Margarite have both failed their managers, but in different ways. What risks do both these managers now face?

The fourth set of questions invites you to analyze the political dynamics following the meeting:

- Lan Xhiao mishandled this meeting from the offset. What should she have done differently and better?

- What should Lan Xhiao's first move be once the meeting is concluded?

- Having promised to get back to Grant and Margarite by the close of business, Lan Xhiao must do so. What should her aim be for this meeting?

Lastly, let's look at the range of political behaviors used by the main characters in the case study.

- Which political behaviors from the examples cited in the previous chapter, or earlier in the book, did Grant, Margarite or Satoshi employ?

LEARNING FROM LAN XHIAO'S MISTAKES

The final section of this chapter provides a summary of the key issues in the case study. Each of the bullet points below relates, in order, to one of the questions above. You might like to read each answer and compare it with the notes that you jotted down. Let's start with the political dynamics involving Lan Xhiao and Satoshi:

- Satoshi operates out of two hidden agendas. What are they?

    Satoshi's first hidden agenda is to avoid conflict or confrontation at any cost. His aversion to conflict is so strong that, when the meeting turns confrontational early on, he opts out, leaving his manager to handle the business unit managers. He only speaks twice, once to answer a question put to him by Lan Xhiao and again to attack the business unit for failing to co-operate with his team. He fails to support his manager even though it is he who has the up-to-date and fuller picture of what's been going on between the business unit and the technology team. Eventually, his discomfort with the confrontational tone of the meeting results in him leaving before it is ended, abandoning his boss to Grant and Margarite.

Satoshi's second hidden agenda is connected to his first. He doesn't tell his manager that there are serious performance issues in the team. He only tells her half the story and lets her think that the picture is rosier than it actually is. His motive here is to let his manager think he is handling his duties better than he actually is, so that he can avoid having to confront the problems in the team that he'd have to tackle if his boss knew the true extent of the team's problems day-to-day. By failing to inform his manager about the true purpose of the meeting, Satoshi sets her up for a fall. This is disastrous for his reputation with his manager and deeply affects the way she perceives him.

- Satoshi tells the business unit managers that their staff have repeatedly failed to co-operate with his team. While this is true, he could have made much better use of these facts in the meeting had he handled them differently. How should he have handled this information?

Firstly, Satoshi should have informed his manager before the meeting about all the ways in which the business unit had failed to co-operate with the technology team. This would have enabled them together to confront Grant and Margarite constructively and help them see their complicity in their own problems. Secondly, Satoshi should not have got into a tit-for-tat debate with Grant. When Grant lists all the faults and failings he perceives to exist with the technology team, either Satoshi or Lan Xhiao could have calmly said, 'Those things may be true or they may not. Let's step back a bit here and find a way forward'. They could then have outlined one instance only of where their team had requested, for example, downtime for maintenance and been turned down. They could have gone on to explain the consequences for the business unit's technology platform of irregular or no maintenance and have asked for co-operation in finding a way forward. Having secured that co-operation, they could have then gone on to cite the next example of non co-operation, perhaps pointing out how much better service they could offer the business unit if they could station two of their teams on the business unit floor and so on. Sadly, by getting into a tit-for-tat argument with Grant, Satoshi plays straight into his hands. Grant wants the meeting to be conducted in an atmosphere of heightened emotion because it enables him to become more forceful – his strong suite. Satoshi isn't good with conflict and his ploy of attacking Grant over the business unit's failure to help his team help them backfires on him.

■ Lan Xhiao is completely taken aback by the business unit's appraisal of her team's performance. Without any facts to go on, and without any support from the largely silent Satoshi, she is wrong-footed. What mistakes does she make in the meeting?

Lan Xhiao's first mistake is to let Grant and Margarite know they have wrong-footed her early on. She does this by asking them, at the start of the meeting, what the purpose of the meeting is, thereby making it appear that she either doesn't know or isn't sure. This puts her on the back foot, and enables the skilled tactician in Grant to go on to the front foot and catalog a series of issues he has with the technology team. Lan Xhiao's second mistake is to ask her number two, in front of Grant and Margarite, if the view they subscribe to is accurate. This is a major miscalculation as it presents her as, firstly, not knowing what is going on in her department, and secondly, makes the lack of unity between her and her team manager apparent to their enemies across the table. Her third error of judgment involves her apologizing and thereby taking responsibility for service failures when she doesn't know for sure that she has anything to apologize for. She has been told by Grant and Margarite that she does, but she doesn't know it for certain without factual proof. Her fourth error is to turn for help to Satoshi a second time in front of her business unit colleagues. This makes her look weak. Her fifth error is to offer to get back to them by the end of the day, an action which means that she has assumed responsibility for sorting out a series of problems which they, really, have contributed to and need to address in tandem with her. Lan Xhiao would have been better off by starting the meeting with a statement like 'what issues do you want to discuss?' She could then have listened to Grant and Margarite's answers. She could have noted the key points down, asked for proof of their claims and, if they couldn't provide any then and there, have offered to reconvene when they could provide some. This would have pre-empted the scapegoating tactics Grant and Margarite used, would have presented the technology team managers as a united pair, and would have sidestepped the slanging match which ensued. This approach would have meant that Lan

Xhiao wouldn't have to go away and work furiously to find something constructive to say by the end of the day.

Let's move on to the second set of questions about the political dynamics involving Grant and Margarite:

■ Where the technology team is concerned, Grant operates out of several hidden agendas. What are they?

Firstly, Grant dislikes being dependent on the technology team, who he thinks of as techies. He blames them, unfairly, for almost anything that goes wrong in his unit that has a technology element to it, whether or not the technology itself is actually at fault. He sees things in black and white terms, and having formed a view, rarely changes it. This combination of factors predisposes Grant to scapegoat the technology team relentlessly and at every opportunity. Secondly, Grant isn't good with detail so, when under pressure in a meeting, he throws his weight around and takes control by heightening the levels of aggression and force he uses to convey his points. He uses both his scapegoating agenda and his aggression agenda throughout the meeting with the technology team.

■ Margarite operates out of a hidden agenda in her relationship with her manager. What is it?

In order to avoid being seen as an ineffective manager Margarite manipulates Grant's perceptions, playing on his well-known personal animosity toward and dislike of technologists. She encourages him to scapegoat them to deflect blame from her own poor management of her group, and its declining standards.

■ At the meeting Margarite is effective at setting her manager up to scapegoat the technology team for its supposed failure to deliver. What issues does this approach raise for her in the future?

This is actually a high-risk strategy for Margarite to adopt. Should Lan Xhiao come back to Grant and Margarite at the end of the day with facts to support Satoshi's assertions that the unit have not co-operated with the technology team, Margarite will be in trouble. *She* will be exposed as the person who hasn't co-operated with the technology team, and as the person who has then encouraged her boss to blame them instead of her. This truth will undermine her fragile alliance with Grant who may see her as manipulative and dishonest. He may well turn on her to protect himself.

Let's move onto the third set of questions about the political dynamics between the business unit and the technology team:

■ Neither the technology team nor the business unit is wholly blameless in this situation. What should each group now do to put things on an even keel?

These two sets of managers need to put aside their differences and work together for the good of their company. In particular, Satoshi and Margarite need to work together to define and then stick to a planned maintenance schedule which allows the technology team to repair and attend to ongoing issues with the business unit's system. The business unit needs to find space for two technologists on their floor so that they can respond immediately to small, but important, requests for assistance from business unit staff. The business unit staff need to stop verbally abusing their technology team colleagues, the lead for which needs to come from their two managers. Margarite, Grant, Lan Xhiai and Satoshi need to have regular, planned update meetings at which to report on and resolve ongoing service delivery issues. Finally, both the business unit and the technology team together need to approach the company's senior managers with facts to support a joint case for technology to have an increased headcount. Their argument for the increased headcount could centre on the fact that their workload has increased significantly since the installation of the 24-hour tracking system. Overall, the four managers need to start to work together, talk to one another, co-operate with one another, and stop blaming each other.

■ Satoshi and Margarite have both failed their managers, but in different ways. What risks do both these managers now face?

Both Satoshi and Margarite face the possibility that their respective managers will see through their political tactics. Lan Xhiao now realizes that Satoshi has only given her half the story to avoid being exposed as less effective than he'd like to be seen as. She may now approach her relationship with him completely differently, managing him more tightly and trusting him less. Grant might realize that Margarite has been managing his perceptions and inciting him to attack and blame the technology team as an alternative to her owning her own poor managerial performance. He may well decide that she cannot be trusted either and might start to take over more of the day-to-day management of the unit.

Let's move onto the fourth set of questions about the political dynamics following the meeting:

- What should Lan Xhiao's first move be once the meeting is concluded?

  Lan Xhiao needs to sit down with Satoshi and get some facts about how often her team have requested downtime, maintenance windows, the option of having staff on the business unit's floor and so on. Lan Xhiao needs to find out the facts of these matters so that she can go to the meeting later that day with solutions and remedies to the issues on the table.

- Having promised to get back to Grant and Margarite by the close of business, Lan Xhiao must do so. What should her aim be for this meeting?

  Her aim must be to present a clear way forward that addresses all the issues Grant and Margarite have put to her. She needs to do this by setting a solutions-focused and collaborative tone, being clear about the extent of the co-operation she needs from the business unit and detailing specific steps she needs them to take to help her help them. These steps might include planned maintenance windows, planned service delivery reviews, ongoing dialog between the two groups and so on.

Lastly, let's look at the range of political behaviors used by the main characters in the case study.

- Which political behaviors from the examples cited in the previous chapter, or earlier in the book, did Grant, Margarite and Satoshi employ?

  Grant and Margarite both employ the tactic of automatic cynicism during the meeting. They don't believe that the technology team will address any of the points they have put to them and say so, with some feeling, claiming that they have heard it all before. Satoshi employs the tactic of verbal withdrawal at the meeting, and eventually, actually leaves it. He does this to avoid having to remain in a conflict which he finds discomforting. Margarite and Grant employ the tactic of scapegoating the technology team throughout the meeting. In Margarite's case this is to deflect attention from her own poor performance in managing her business unit; and in Grant's case it is because he habitually scapegoats technology if he can and, in this case, has been incited to do so by his number two. Grant's threat to call Lan Xhiao's boss in Hong Kong is an example of escalating a conflict. He threatens not to respect her right to handle the issues he is putting to her, and suggests escalating matters upwards simply to flex his muscles, not because he is justified in doing so. Satoshi's list of reasons why his team haven't provided the standard of service the business unit expect *sounds like* a series of justifications for failure to deliver to the business unit because of the way in which he frames and delivers the information. And finally, as noted above, Satoshi, Grant and Margarite all operate out of different hidden agendas before and during the meeting.

This case study has focused on a situation in which a number two in a business unit decides to cover up her own shortcomings as a manager by inciting her own manager to scapegoat their colleagues in technology. She does this in an attempt to cloud over the real issues behind their unit's poor business performance. The case study has also highlighted how vulnerable the technology manager is to this ploy because she has delegated the day-to-day management of her team to her number two, a man who doesn't handle conflict well and doesn't tell his manager the whole story. It has illustrated how challenging it can be to respond effectively to the political tactic of scapegoating unless you have the full facts at your fingertips. The case study demonstrates how essential it is to unearth personal agendas and manage the political dynamics in a meeting at the time they occur, rather than trying to revisit them afterwards. It also highlights how important it is to refocus a contentious debate around solutions rather than letting it get bogged down in blame shifting, lying and scapegoating.

The following, and last, chapter of the book concludes our discussion of how to identify and handle political behavior in your workplace. Its aim is to focus your mind on four key points as you apply the material from this book to your workplace relationships.

Final Thoughts

YOUR EXPERIENCES OF WORKPLACE POLITICS

Every one of you will have stories to tell about workplace politics: how people you trusted let you down, how you misread the political motives of some of your colleagues, how you were surprised by the political intentions of colleagues you had previously judged to be non-political, how you failed to understand who had influence over which aspect of a key decision or how you couldn't find colleague support for your preferred outcome over a particular decision. You'll have many other variations on these themes as well. Each of you will also have stories to tell of situations where you used your political management skills effectively to get things done: where you made sound judgments about which more influential colleagues to approach for support over a particular issue, where you worked long and hard to presell your proposals to other colleagues and formed effective and influential alliances, where you handled the controlling behaviors of colleagues effectively or where you successfully confronted someone who tried to take your personal power from you. You'll have many variations on these themes too, but, at the end of the day, it's what you learn from the situations that haven't gone your way that will enable you to identify and handle similar dynamics differently and better in the future.

YOUR POLITICAL MANAGEMENT SKILLS

My aim in writing this book is to give you some tools, skills, insight, tactics and wisdom that will enable you to navigate the political territory in your workplace more effectively. But, at the end of the day, it's your application of the material, tools and ideas in this book to your day-to-day workplace relationships that will make the difference. To do this effectively you will need to:

- Work methodically toward your own role goals at all times.
- Look at your own political conduct through the eyes of your colleagues from time to time.

- Ensure that each and every time you seek to have influence in a situation you think involves political elements, you take the time to consider the full range of the dynamics at play before you act.
- Manage yourself, your time and your energy so that you make sound decisions about which political issues to tackle and which to leave to those better placed to handle them than you.

YOUR POLITICAL EXPERIENCES

I'd like very much to hear about your experiences of identifying and handling political behavior in your workplace. The following page will provide you with details about how to get in touch with me. Whatever sector you work in, whatever your role or your level of seniority, I hope that reading this book has equipped you with a more effective set of strategies for handling workplace politics, and has increased your confidence and skill at stepping into terrain you consider to be political. I hope that reading this book will prove to be a catalyst that enables you to develop your political skills sufficiently so that you enjoy your work more, gain the profile you want to have and develop the influence you'd like to have over the workplace issues that matter most to you.

Above all, I hope that reading this book will enable you to put your energy and enthusiasm toward the part of your work that you most enjoy, and that less and less of your time and effort will be dissipated in ineffective responses to other people's political behavior.

Aryanne Oade

To tell me about your experiences of identifying and managing political behavior in your workplace, or to explore options to help you develop further political skills visit www.oadeassociates.com.

References and Recommended Reading

REFERENCES

Chapter 4   Tool Two: The Politics of Values and Styles

A. Oade (2009) *Starting and Running a Coaching Business: The Complete Guide to Setting Up and Managing a Coaching Practice* (Oxford: How To Books) ISBN 978-1-84528-332-2.

E. T. Robinson (1995) *Why Aren't You More Like Me? Styles and Skills for Leading and Living with Credibility*, HRD Press ISBN 970-0-87425-970-3.

Chapter 6   Tool Three: The Political Roles People Play: Getting Things Done With Others

Tuckner Consulting Inc. has a framework which uses some of the same concepts as the one I present in this chapter. Details of their framework can be found at the following link:
http://www.mncn.org/EventMaterial/2008Ldrshp/InfluencingStratTuckner.pdf.

Chapter 8   Tool Four: Power and Politics: Bringing Your Plans to Fruition

J. R. P. French Jr and B. Raven (1959) 'The Bases of Social Power', in D. Cartwright (ed.) *Studies in Social Power* (Ann Arbor: University of Michigan, Institute for Social Research) pp. 150–67. For an update on French and Raven's work see D. E. Frost and A. J. Stahleski (1988) 'The Systematic Measurement of French and Raven's Bases of Social Power in Workgroups', *Journal of Applied Social Psychology*, April, pp. 375–89.

Chapter 10   Tool Five: Objective Criteria for Assessing Trusting Behavior

P. Drucker (1997) 'Managing in a Time of Great Change', *HR Alliances*, 1 (1), pp. 1–2, quoted in *Trust: The Ultimate Test* L. R. Libove and

E. M. Russo (1997) HRDQ, Organisation Design and Development Inc.

R. C. Mayer, J. H. Davies and F. D. Schoorman (1995) 'An Integrative Model of Organisational Trust', *Academy of Management Review*, 20 (3), pp. 709–34.

M. Sinetar (1988) 'Building Trust into Corporate Relationships', *Organisational Dynamics*, 16 (3), pp. 73–9.

L. R. Libove and E. M. Russo (1997) *Trust: The Ultimate Test* HRDQ, Organisation Design and Development Inc.

RECOMMENDED READING

L. R. Libove and E. M. Russo (1997) *Trust: The Ultimate Test* HRDQ, Organisation Design and Development Inc.

This questionnaire booklet is an interesting synopsis of research on trust at work, and includes an effective trust questionnaire which you can self-score.

Everett T. Robinson (1995) *Why Aren't You More Like Me? Styles and Skills for Leading and Living with Credibility*, HRD Press ISBN 970-0-87425-970-3.

There are a number of behavioral styles models on the market, with related books and materials. This paperback book is a thorough, informative and readable examination of one of the more comprehensive behavioral styles theories, Personal Style Indicator, by one of its co-authors.

Index